Kouthwou Chang

P9-EKS-483

PLAIN
TALK
ON
Genesis

PLAIN TALK ON

Genesis

MANFORD GEORGE GUTZKE

**ZONDERVAN
PUBLISHING HOUSE** OF THE ZONDERVAN CORPORATION
GRAND RAPIDS, MICHIGAN 49506

PLAIN TALK ON GENESIS
Copyright © 1975 by The Zondervan Corporation
Grand Rapids, Michigan

Library of Congress Catalog Card Number: 74-25330

All rights reserved. No part of this publication may be reproduced, stored
in a retrieval system, or transmitted in any form or by any means—electronic,
mechanical, photocopy, recording or otherwise—without the prior permission
of the copyright owner, except for brief quotations in reviews.

Printed in the United States of America

CONTENTS

PREFACE

This study is written from the point of view of a Christian reading the Old Testament. The purpose will be to seek insight for a clearer understanding of the truth in Christ as set forth in the New Testament. There will not be any conscious attempt to persuade any doubting heart that this is the Word of God, but there will be a deliberate effort to see the truth revealed in this Scripture and to understand how it can and will affect the one who is reading and studying. "To know Christ and to make Him known" is frankly and openly our ambition.

The Book of Genesis will be the subject of our study, but we will deal with this Scripture as a part of the Bible. Our attitude toward the Bible as a whole will be the attitude we will maintain in dealing with Genesis. We have in mind that when Jesus of Nazareth lived He used the Old Testament Scriptures that He might present the Word of God. The Book of Genesis which we have in our hands today is substantially the same as the text He had when He quoted the Scriptures. There is not one instance of any record that He ever contradicted or changed any part of the record as it is written. As we read Genesis today we can be satisfied we are reading just what He read when He taught in the synagogue.

When Jesus of Nazareth began His public ministry, He was referred to as the one "of whom Moses and the prophets did write." In the Hebrew Scriptures at the time Jesus of Nazareth lived, the first five books of the Bible were spoken of as "the books of Moses." What we now call "Genesis" was known as "the first book of Moses." Thus we read in Luke 24:27, "And beginning at Moses and all the prophets, he expounded unto them in all the scriptures the things concerning himself." Therefore we take up the Book of Genesis with special interest, because this is where Christ Jesus began when He was teaching the truth about Himself.

We realize that today many students have many reservations in heart and in mind when they read in the Old Testament, and especially when they read Genesis, "as it is written." We remind ourselves that we have the very text which was read by Jesus of Nazareth, and we remember there is not one iota of evidence that He ever showed any reservation about any part of it. Paul said that he worshiped "the God of my fathers, believing all things which are written in the law and in the prophets." We have no hesitation to commit ourselves publicly to the fullest confidence in the Scripture "as it is written" and are persuaded that such an attitude enables us to learn more fully what is revealed in the written "Word of God."

It is possible that some more sophisticated minds will find this "Plain Talk" somewhat less challenging to their intellects, because every effort has been made to expound the meaning in simple, clear terms. I do not need to try to express the whole truth of the Word of God: that has been done in the Scriptures themselves. I have the task of so discussing this written truth in such language, using the vernacular in such a way that those who are not acquainted with the whole body of Scripture might be able to grasp some of the truth revealed in this portion. Let it be sufficient that I realize such may want to read elsewhere, but let me strive to present what I have to say in such "Plain Talk" that "the wayfaring men, though fools, shall not err therein" (Isa. 35:8).

The Basis of Our Approach to Bible Study

We have the Bible

The Bible as it is has been placed in our hands by Providence. Written centuries ago by about forty authors, many of whom are actually unknown to us, and copied again and again in longhand script by unknown persons, this Book of books has been published and distributed over the earth in more than 1,000 languages and dialects.

We accept the Bible

We know the Bible has been criticized by active, brilliant minds who have suspiciously examined the text expecting to find evidence to discredit the material as being untrue to facts of history or science. We know also that archaeological research at great expense has been carried on to discover facts that might contradict the historical records in the Bible. Despite the obscurity of the origin of the manuscripts comprising the Bible, the records remain unshaken. This is our text.

We trust the Bible

There are things written in the Bible we cannot explain or understand. But this is no different from the situation we face in science, in medicine, and in engineering. Every day we exercise trust in devices, in mechanisms, in professional servants of society, involving commitment of fortune and welfare even to life itself. In doing this we act with intelligence, because we have good reason to trust these men and these machines. In the same way we feel we are acting with intelligence when we trust the Bible: we have good reason to do so.

We honor the Bible

The Bible has been involved in and associated with so much that is good and helpful to mankind. Its supporters and promoters have been persons of integrity, many of them eminent in character. The Bible has served to comfort and to strengthen many souls in their darkest hours of deepest distress. It has meant and does mean so much in the world that we approach our study with that deference in spirit which we believe to be simply its honest due.

We believe the Bible

Therefore we read it carefully and study it respectfully with the aim to learn what it says and to understand what it means, for us in our own daily lives. We expect that many of the puzzling problems of life in the world today can be understood and dealt with in the light of Bible truth. So we seek to see clearly what the Bible means, and then to speak to all the world with plain talk about Bible truth for everyday living.

PLAIN
TALK
ON
Genesis

Chapter One

INTRODUCTION

Every human being at one time or another realizes that he is living in a dangerous world. We live day by day in circumstances beyond our control. It is the things we do or leave undone that make a difference. We can be hurt or we can be pleased. All around us are some things that are helpful and some that are hurtful. We cannot be certain whether the things we do will bring success or failure, but because we do not want to be losers we learn all we can. We develop our skills in every possible way, and do the very best to get as far as we can. We do not want to be like fish in a flowing river, and yet the truth is that if we do not swim, the current will carry us away. Everything around us is frightening until we realize the wonderful truth that we are not alone: this world was created by God.

We were created by God. Events as they occur are not happenstance. They are controlled and supervised by God. Life is meaningful and purposeful since we have been persuaded personally that God is, and that He is Almighty. There are people who do not believe this, but their unbelief does not change anything. I am satisfied that the things I know in my heart, and which I am ready to share with others, could be a matter of living successfully or of being swept out to sea.

God is not only the Creator who controls and supervises all things, but He has put into our hands an inspired book, which we call the Bible or the Word of God. The Bible speaks of God in relation to the world in which we live, in relation to man, and in relation to the future. The Bible talks about these things. It tells us in unmistakable words that God is in charge and in control. He is sovereign. He rules supreme. He made nature as it is and man as he is. He gave to each one of us a conscience. He gave us the natural processes as they exist, and the Ten Commandments as they are written.

Then, too, the Bible tells us that God is the keeper and sustainer of the world which He created. We call His ways Providence. There is a sentence in the New Testament which touches my heart each time I read it. It tells that God's eye is on the sparrow. Not one sparrow falls to the ground but that He sees it (Matt. 10:29). God knows everything and watches over everything.

The Bible also tells us that God is just and holy. God not only evaluates everything but He judges everything. Our conscience would tell us this and so does the Bible. In addition we find in the Scripture the wonderful news that God is gracious and merciful to people who do not deserve it, and will save those who come to Him, trusting in His promises. These promises are revealed in the Bible.

There are various translations of the Bible, but this is not important. No matter which version we read, Christ walked on the water in each one of them. He opened the eyes of the blind in each one. He brought Lazarus to life in each one, and He went to the cross of Calvary in each version, and He arose from the dead in each version we read. The multiple narratives of the same event as recorded in the four gospels do not change the facts. There is no real barrier there. There is never any contradiction.

The names of the gospel writers or of the authors of other books of the Bible are not important. It is what is in the books that counts. It is like medicine. The name of the pharmacist who made up the prescription does not matter; it's the medicine that matters. So it is the Bible that matters. It is what is in the Bible that will really bless our souls.

In the Book of Genesis, the beginning of life in this world is set forth. Here we have the record of the creation of the world as it was created and made by God. This will include the amazing consistency of things. We take it for granted that everything will stay as it is. Salt will remain salt, and sugar will remain sugar. Water will always be water and fire will be fire. Iron will remain iron, and hydrogen will remain hydrogen. The earth will be like the earth and rocks will be rocks, and none of this will ever vary. It is always true that after the sowing of the seed comes the fruit. Everything happens in order. We may say, "That's only natural," but do we ever stop to ask who made this "natural" business? It is God!

The reliability and the steadfastness of all things is far more important than we ever imagine. When we think of the ground being steady under our feet, do we ever realize how important this is? Those of us who have lived through an earthquake can realize this fully. I was in Los Angeles on such an occasion, when the earth began to shake. It happened after dark at night. In no time at all the streets were filled with screaming people. It was just that way! It was a terrifying thing to see and hear and feel.

I realized then so clearly that only the power of God who created the world keeps it in its place. God not only called the world into being, but He is in control of it. In His providence the sun will shine and the rain will fall. The natural processes go on because God is faithful. He neither slumbers nor sleeps; He does not grow weary. He holds the whole wide world in His hand!

As He judges the earth, God blesses and destroys. Many will say, "I can't believe that God would ever destroy anything that He made." But the Bible tells us that God will destroy in judgment. As we look about us we see this illustrated in nature. We see grass growing and we know it will die. We watch flowers growing and we know that they will wither. Everything in nature will eventually be destroyed.

The Bible tells of man's plight as he faces his doom, but also of the mercy of God which will save man from destruction. The Bible shows that man is guilty and is moving headlong toward God's judgment and condemnation. Man is sinful. Deep down in his heart man does not want to do what is right. He wants to do as he pleases, and this is the sinful condition that will ruin him unless checked.

The Book of Genesis will tell us of the judgment of God which destroys and of the grace of God which is a free gift. We will find in the Book of Genesis the truth about the condition of mankind. "There is a way that seemeth right with a man, but the ends thereof are the ways of death." We will see that because God is holy and just, He judges that which is evil and sinful. But to His glory it will be shown that He actually offers help to sinful man. He offers to save and to cleanse any defiled person, and promises to bless all who trust in Him.

The last thirty-nine chapters of Genesis are to a great extent the history of four men, commonly called the Patriarchs. First we read about Abraham, the father of the faithful. In studying the life of Abraham, we can see what living by faith actually means. When God called him, Abraham went out "not knowing whither he went," because he knew God! The second of the Patriarchs is Isaac, about whom much could be said, but nothing greater than the one thing which we may call "the wisdom of Isaac." The third of these pioneers of faith is Jacob, whose name was changed to Israel. This man became the father of the twelve tribes of Israel. The fourth Patriarch about whom we shall study is Joseph, who was a very wonderful person and beloved in the sight of God.

Before beginning a detailed study of the Book of Genesis, it might be well to look at the language in which the book is written. We are living in a time of many modern translations of the Scriptures into everyday language. It is of course important that the Scriptures be easily understood, but it is far more important that the message that is taught and preached be truly and accurately reported. Since God is invisible and His ways are past finding out, there is a temptation to recast the Scriptures in concepts that are our own, so that they can be more credible. But we must beware of the grave danger here of using our own ideas so that what we say, while more readily understandable, may not be true to the original record. For this reason it is very important to know something of the original Hebrew language in which the Book of Genesis was written.

Many of us do not speak the language of the Old Testament, but scholars can and have mastered it. Let us look at a few interesting things about the Hebrew language. Nearly all the words which are used in Hebrew are verbal forms; that is, they are forms of some verbs. These are action words. There are not many nouns. Actually there are only about 900 verbs used in the whole Hebrew language. By far the most of the words are made up from these roots. Another interesting feature is that these verbs have no tenses. There is nothing in the form of the verb that will show whether the action indicated means something that was past or something that is present, or something that is future. Hebrew verbs have just two ways of describing action. The particular action being referred to is either going on or it is finished. In other words, the imperfect state of the action, or the perfect state of the action, is all that is shown. Thus you are never told by the text itself whether this happened 1,000 years ago, is happening now, or will happen 1,000 years from now.

While the verbs have no tenses, and that seems to be almost too simple, they do use seven voices. In our English language we speak of "active voice" and "passive voice." In the Greek there are three voices: the active voice, the middle voice, and the passive voice. The seven voices in Hebrew enable the writer to use seven different ways in referring to any action. For example, in speaking English to refer to the action of "killing," I could say "I kill": that would be in the active voice. If I said "I was killed" I would be using the passive voice. If I were using Greek I could have three voices. I could say "I kill." Or I could say "I was killed" and also I could say "I killed myself." In the Greek these three voices would each use a different form of the verb. But in the Hebrew, I could have seven voices. I could say "I kill"; and I could say "I was killed." Then I could say "I massacred," i.e., "I just killed and killed and killed intensively." Then I could say "I was massacred. I was slaughtered," meaning to say I was killed violently. Then I could say "I caused to kill." There is a special verb form for that. Then I could say "I was caused to kill. Someone else made me do it." And finally I could say "I committed suicide." I have labored this point to show the Hebrew language is capable of reporting many variations of the manner of any action.

It is interesting to note that Hebrew is the language of creation. Some of the words that are used in the Book of Genesis are very meaningful. The word for God, in Genesis, is *Elohim*. There are other Hebrew words for God. But this particular word means the "Strong One." That is literally what the word means in Hebrew. *Elohim* is "the one with energy." He is the Creator. Today our scientists tell us that all matter (all items as they occur) is basically some form of energy. The Hebrew language fits in with this when it says in Genesis that the "Great Energy One" is the One who created the heavens and the earth.

Another illustration can be seen in the Hebrew word *rakiah*, translated as "firmament" in Genesis 1:6. Far from implying anything "firm," as would have suited the ideas of the Egyptians, Greeks or Romans, the Hebrew word actually means "expanse" or "expansion," which is almost exactly what we mean today by "space." And so the Hebrew language again is seen to be amazingly suitable to describe the natural world in line with our best observation of today.

Chapter Two

THE DAYS OF CREATION

(Genesis 1)

The Apostles' Creed speaks of the creation: "I believe in God the Father, Almighty, Maker of heaven and earth." In the German language the Apostles' Creed affirms, "I believe in God the Father, Almighty, Creator of heaven and earth"; and this is actually more carefully true. "In the beginning God created the heaven and the earth." In Genesis 1:21 it is written: "God created great whales, and every living creature that moveth, which the waters brought forth abundantly, after their kind, and every winged fowl after his kind." In verse 27 these words are recorded: "So God created man in his own image, in the image of God created he him; male and female created he them." Here the word *created* is found three times in one verse. The verb *create* is rarely found in the Hebrew text. It is found more often in Genesis 1 than anywhere else in the Old Testament. The word means "to bring into existence out of nothing."

The word *make* is frequently used in the Old Testament and means "to construct out of materials already in hand." A dressmaker does not make the cloth, nor the thread, but she takes the materials and makes the dress. In the same way a shoemaker takes leather, cutting it and shaping it into a shoe out of material in hand. Romans 4:17 says about God: "Who . . . called those things which be not as though they were." In other words, God calls them into existence. Man makes things out of available material. An architect designs a building. He gets together brick, stone, steel,

19

glass, and all other items that are needed for the building. In the same way a milliner designs a hat and uses ready materials for making it.

An architect creates the design, but he cannot call a cathedral into being. He must use the materials to construct the building. Only God can create materials. Only He can call into existence those things which "be not."

Genesis 1:2 states: "And the earth was without form, and void; and darkness was upon the face of the deep. And the spirit of God moved upon the face of the waters." In reading these words one can almost feel the dense black darkness, the lifeless, lightless chaos which they picture. The words *moved upon* can be better translated "brooded over." The verb that is used has in it the idea of wings. It could be said the Spirit of God was "winging" over the face of the waters, hovering over, fluttering over, brooding over, as a hen broods over the eggs which she is hatching.

Beginning at Genesis 1:3-5 is found the record of the great happenings of each succeeding day in the creation event: "And God said, Let there be light: and there was light. And God saw the light, that it was good: and God divided the light from the darkness. And God called the light Day, and the darkness he called Night. And the evening and the morning were the first day."

This light has been called cosmic light, because apparently it did not come from the sun, since God did not call the sun into being until the fourth day. This cosmic light was everywhere. If light is understood as a form of energy, it could be everywhere. Not all light comes from the sun. Light comes from the stars, and light as moving energy is to be found all through the heavens. No one knows what light is. It has been referred to as "moving points of energy." That sounds good but no one knows what energy is. Actually light is something that we cannot define or know. Even when we are told that it travels by waves we might ask, waves of what? No one knows why it seems to appear in undulating form, in the manner of waves. We still have no idea what is undulating, or what causes it to move.

Genesis 1:6-8 states, "And God said, Let there be a firmament in the midst of the waters, and let it divide the waters from the waters. And God made the firmament, and divided the waters which were under the firmament from the waters which were above the firmament: and it was so. And God called the firmament Heaven. And the evening and the morning were the second day." The word *firmament* is interesting because it seems to be based upon the idea of something "firm," which is misleading. At the time when this Bible was translated into Latin, the general view of the universe was that the whole sky was a dome over the earth. This dome was considered to be like a great canopy over the whole earth. The stars were thought of as shafts of light which pierced this blue dome. But the original Hebrew word *rakiah* in no way implies anything solid, but rather means "expanding space." That this word was used in the Hebrew can only be accounted for by divine revelation, because at the time when Genesis was written, the thought of Egypt dominated the Western world, and their great philosopher, Ptolemy, taught that the heavens were solid. It is interesting to note that the Hebrew idea of "expanding space" is as modern as the latest concept so far as the universe is concerned.

Genesis 1:9-13 records:

> And God said, Let the waters under the heaven be gathered together unto one place, and let the dry land appear: and it was so. And God called the dry land Earth; and the gathering together of the waters called he Seas: and God saw that it was good. And God said, Let the earth bring forth grass, the herb yielding seed, and the fruit tree yielding fruit after his kind, whose seed is in itself, upon the earth: and it was so. And the earth brought forth grass, and herb yielding seed after his kind, and the tree yielding fruit, whose seed was in itself, after his kind: and God saw that it was good. And the evening and the morning were the third day.

Thus on the third day two happenings occurred. First there was the gathering of the waters into "seas," and the appearing of dry land which was called "earth." Then there came forth "the grass and herbs." There again it is of interest as a matter of language to note that in the Hebrew the word for "grass" actually means "sproutage," everything that comes out of the ground in sprouts. The trees also with seed bearing fruit for reproduction appeared on the third day. It may be noted that the one distinguishing trait about such plants was that they "yielded seed" that would reproduce "after their kind."

Genesis 1:14-19 records the creating of our solar system:

> And God said, Let there be lights in the firmament of the heaven to divide the day from the night; and let them be for signs, and for seasons, and for days, and years: And let them be for lights in the firmament of the heaven to give light upon the earth: and it was so. And God made two great lights; the greater light to rule the day, and the lesser light to rule the night: he made the stars also. And God set them in the firmament of the heaven to give light upon the earth, and to rule over the day and over the night, and to divide the light from the darkness: and God saw that it was good. And the evening and the morning were the fourth day.

The word *light* in the Hebrew implies "light holders" or "light reflectors." This is most interesting because it suggests that the sun does not originate light, even though the light comes from the sun to us with the solar bodies as some sort of reflectors. In any case, whatever light is, God created certain solar bodies that were to be reflectors of light, so that they would control our system of times, seasons, days, and years.

Genesis 1:20-23 records the origin of birds and fish:

> And God said, Let the waters bring forth abundantly the moving creature that hath life, and fowl that may fly above the earth in the open firmament of heaven. And God created great whales, and every living creature that moveth, which the waters brought forth abundantly, after their kind, and every winged fowl after his kind: and God saw that it was good. And God blessed them, saying, Be fruitful, and multiply, and fill the waters in the seas, and let fowl multiply in the earth. And the evening and the morning were the fifth day.

And so at last the earth was ready for the creation of man, who would be given authority to have dominion over all creatures.

Genesis 1:24-31 records what happened on the sixth day, when God created animals and man. Here is the simple account of how God created man in His own image and gave him the capacity to exercise rule over the earth.

In this whole account of creation the amazing thing is that the order in which God created the universe, as it is written, exactly fits the best thinking of scientists today as to when these various items actually came into existence. When this record is compared to the views current among the pagans of that time and culture, the impression is astonishing and amazing.

At this point some consideration would seem to be in order which would deal with the harmful theory of "evolution." It is a natural thing to wonder how the universe came into being. The Bible tells us plainly that "God created the heaven and the earth," but not everyone believes or even knows the Scriptures. In different parts of the world people have held various ideas about the origin of life in this world. Throughout the centuries men have speculated how this universe came into being. Many theories appeal to the natural mind which are based upon natural processes, with the general idea that all organisms developed from one source. Many will claim that civilized man as we know him today was once a savage, who in turn was a cave man, who in turn probably descended from apes or monkeys. Such thinkers illustrate their ideas in textbooks and in museums by using their imagination. They often go back in their own speculation to some assumed original one-celled protoplasm dwelling in primordial ooze from which they claim that by natural processes more complex forms evolved. This general theory can then be used to propose that all life forms started originally as simple one-celled creatures which then developed and developed through successive generations until more complex organisms appeared in time. This is a simple sketch of what is commonly called "evolution."

Such a view as this implies that in nature itself there is some upward thrust that has produced man, who in himself is therefore some superior kind of animal. There are of course many versions of this so-called theory of evolution, and some of these versions as they are offered actually propose to include God as the creative force. Some theorists want to hold to a type of evolution without discarding the opening chapter of Genesis altogether. This of course is quite impossible, because it is not at all what the Bible teaches.

The Genesis account as it is written is as plain as day: it is clearly stated that God by His Word called into being the world and everything in it. Genesis 1:3 records simply: "Let there be light: and there was light." It does not imply that this light was made of something else. The words do not explain the origin of light. The account simply records: "And there was light," in response to God's command. Genesis 1:6 tells of the creation of space. There is no explanation of how God arranged it. There is only the record: "And God said, Let there be a firmament." Then in verse 7 there is the simple record, "And God made the firmament." There is no description of how this was done beyond the Word of God. Genesis 1:9 states: "And God said . . . Let the dry land appear." There is no description of any process by which this took place. There is no reference to various kinds of erosion, or of upheavals caused by the cooling of the earth's surface. The appearance of the dry land was a function of the will of God. He spoke and it was so. Genesis 1:11 states: "And God said, Let the earth bring forth grass." There is no description of where it came from, only the record that it was there. Genesis 1:14 states: "And God said, Let there be lights in the firmament." Again there is no explanation of this origin of the solar system.

Today man has reached the moon, but this is a very short distance so far as the solar system is concerned. Scientists estimate that it takes thousands, even millions of years for the light from some stars to reach the earth, but the Bible simply records that the heavenly bodies appeared at the Word of God. In Genesis 1:20, 21 there is the account of the creation of all marine and bird life, with the statement, "God saw that it was good." Nothing is stated about their origin, beyond the record that it was the Word of God that called them into being. This is the form of the record over and over. "And God said, Let the earth bring forth the living creatures." "And God said, Let us make man in our image." All these phases of creation are implied in Hebrews 11:3. "Through faith we understand that the worlds were framed by the word of God, so that things which are seen were not made of things which do appear." The Scriptures state plainly that when the Word of God was spoken, there occurred immediately the original creation.

The record of the Scriptures is very clear. It was God's Word that brought things to pass. God spoke and it stood fast. Short and simple as the record is written, there is careful reporting to guard against any possible misunderstanding that the creation as recorded in Genesis happened as a result of natural processes. There seems to be special care to avoid any ground for thinking of natural development. We read again and again in verses 11 to 25, in referring to seed for reproduction, the words "after his kind." In fact they appear ten times in fifteen verses. Eight times we read "after his kind," and twice we find the words "after their kind." Every single plant, every animal, all marine life, and all bird life had this characteristic: each reproduced after "his kind," each one emphasizing a continuity of its own kind. It could seem as though the Holy Spirit, looking into future years when man would doubt the Word of God, inspired the writers of this passage of Scripture to emphasize and to stress the fact that all living matter would reproduce "after its own kind."

It is most important that this aspect of continuity in kind be recognized in creation, because this is basic to all morality. Such constancy is grounded in the very integrity of God, who will keep the order of things "after their own kind." It is well-known that there are different-sized horses, and different-sized dogs, that can be trained and developed differently, but when all is said and done, a horse is a horse, a cow is a cow, and a dog is a dog. This constancy in kind rejects such a theory of "evolution."

Under God it will never be true that evil may be done and good will follow. This is untrue and it is demoralizing:

humanly speaking, nothing can come from nothing but nothing. It is a very serious thing today to have people drift away from absolute standards and talk about relative goodness. It may be quite true that circumstances alter cases, just as there are varieties of wheat and barley and there are varieties of peaches: but it is most important that there be no dilution of this truth; so far as human beings are concerned, the law of the harvest must prevail: "Whatsoever a man soweth, that shall he also reap."

Chapter Three

THE CREATION OF MAN

(Genesis 2)

When a man thinks that he was created by God in the image of God, his outlook upon life and his estimate of himself is profoundly affected. If a man feels that he originally came from the hands of God, and then sees himself breaking God's law, he is humbled. On the other hand if a man were to think he was originally an animal, and had come this far, he would feel pride in himself. He would be tempted to say in his heart, "See how far I have come. There is no stopping me now! I'll go to the very top!" As a matter of fact, the popular theories of evolution and the Bible account of the creation are diametrically opposed to one another. So it follows: a person must choose which to believe. They cannot both be true. Further study of the Book of Genesis will show this very clearly.

Genesis simply records that God created the heavens and the earth, and all things that are therein. This same record states that God created man also. God is eternal. He is infinite. That takes Him beyond our comprehension, but we believe when we read that "God is, and He is a rewarder of them that diligently seek Him." The Bible gives the account of the creation of the world and of man though not the details of procedures involved, and yet it very significantly points out without any question that this is the work of God.

The record is that man was created "in the image of God." The word *image* is an interesting word. In the

Hebrew language that word *image* means "shadow." When my shadow falls on the ground, I know that it is mine and that it differs from all others. Shadows may be long or short, broad or thin. The shadow is dependent upon the reality. As I walk in the sunlight, a creature of flesh and blood, my shadow falls on the grass or on the pavement or on the sand. Obviously this does not mean that I am made of sand or pavement or grass. It just means that my general outline is to be seen there on the ground. And it is my general outline without any details. My shadow is not the same as I am.

When Genesis records that man was created in the likeness of God, this does not mean that the physical structure of man reflects God. It is man's personality traits that in some measure reflect the reality of God. For example, man is able to think up new things. He can be creative and make things that were never seen before. He can improve things. He can judge and recognize right from wrong. Man can invent things. Something of the nature of man can be seen by comparing animals. It has been noted in observing birds that if one were to take a robin's egg and put it into a sparrow's nest, the egg would be hatched as a robin, and while that bird may never have observed any other robins, it will, when it grows to maturity, build a robin's nest. It will build its own nest just as all robins do, and it will never change or improve it. Robins' nests, swallows' nests, and eagles' nests have not changed or improved throughout time. The way a rabbit digs in the ground and the way a wolf finds his den have not been improved in all the generations of animals. Only man has this creative capacity which sets him apart from the animal world and in its measure indicates a likeness to the Creator.

When some students note that the creation of man is described both in chapter 1 and in chapter 2, they speak of two accounts of the creation of man. These need not be taken as different accounts. As a matter of fact in chapter 1 the record is that man was created by God to have dominion over the earth. In chapter 2 appears the classic statement: "The Lord God formed man of the dust of the ground, and breathed into his nostrils the breath of life; and man became a living soul." This sketches the tripartite, the threefold nature of man: body, spirit, and soul. The flesh was made of dust, the spirit is from God who gave it, and the soul occurs in the union. Sometimes the Bible speaks of man as having body, soul, and spirit; and sometimes it refers to two elements in man as soul and body. Living is thought of as a matter of keeping body and soul together.

It may be noted at this point that plants, trees, and flowers are never spoken of in the Bible as being "alive." There are "green" trees spoken of, and "dry" trees. Trees are not spoken of as having life. The Bible teaches that "the life is in the blood." Only man is spoken of as having a spirit which comes from God.

The Genesis account of the creation of man is an ennobling, inspiring record. It shows man as created in the image of God. For a man to think of himself as an animal is debasing. Then he can blame every selfish, unreasonable tendency in himself on the fact that this is the animal nature coming out in him. This tends to lead to unchecked immorality.

Genesis records that God completed the creation in six days, but even more important than accepting and believing that God is the Creator of the universe is the realization of God's relation to this world and to man. Even in this first chapter of Genesis the very clear and very profound truth appears that God not only created the world but He keeps it and judges it. Even so with man: the conduct of man in his relationship with the sovereign God affects his whole destiny.

The story in Genesis goes on to say that God rested on the seventh day. "And God blessed the seventh day, and sanctified it." Man was to appreciate the fact that while activity is important, there is to be a time when work must cease. Man who works is to rest, and that brings a new idea into focus. Some have the idea that work is part of the curse which was pronounced on Adam and his descendants. This is not the truth. The fact that man was to labor would never hurt him. Adam's punishment was that he should labor with difficulty: "in the sweat of thy face." The earth would now bring forth briars and thorns, and it would not be easy to cultivate the ground. This is what belongs to the curse upon man because of his sin.

Work in itself is not necessarily a burden, and can actually bring with it a sense of physical well-being. Sometimes work is a pleasure because of the ensuing results. Then too when work is done for those who are loved, work is never burdensome. It can however become a weariness to the flesh when there are difficulties, such as insects and pests and weeds and thistles and thorns. Anyone who has been bone-tired from working knows how wonderful it is to have a period of rest. I can remember when I was working in the field on a hot day how welcome rest stops were. *Rest* is a wonderful word.

The word *Sabbath* means "seventh": the seventh day, the seventh week, the seventh month, the seventh season, and the seventh group of years. In the Hebrew this word *Sabbath* or "seventh" has a twofold meaning. It not only means "seventh," but it also means "rest"; because it is the day God instituted as a day of rest. By the way, the word *seven* in this context does not mean "seventh" only in a series like 1, 2, 3, 4, 5, 6, 7, but the "seventh" in proportion. "One" out of every "seven." Sabbath always means "rest." When the Scriptures speak of letting the land have its "sabbath," the idea is that farmers should let the land "rest." The law of Moses gave guidance in this matter of agriculture. Every seventh year the land would be left idle, or as it is called "fallow." That was known as the sabbath year.

The rest being discussed is not a matter of inactivity. It is not a matter of sitting still and not doing anything. To be sure for those who have been really busy, running from pillar to post and feeling all worn out, it is a wonderful thing just to sit still and not do anything. However, rest does not need to be silence, because there can be silence without rest. Rest actually means something peaceful with no strain. Rest is the opposite from trouble and tribulation and disturbance.

The Bible tells of God's will that all His people should rest periodically. It is a familiar commandment, "Remember the Sabbath day to keep it holy." In the course of living, men may encounter many strange and new situations, just as the people of Israel did in their long journey in the desert. On the Sabbath day the activities of men were to be suspended. It is to be a day when work ceases, and is to be a reward for work well done.

What a wonderful anticipation this can be for all who labor. Even the hardest, most tiring work is more bearable when the worker can look forward to the day of rest, every seventh day. It has been said that sin broke the rest God intended for all men, but when God sent His Son to redeem men from sin, He restored rest. In the Book of Hebrews we read, "there remaineth therefore a rest to the people of God." In His complete salvation the weary soul finds rest, and the troubled soul finds peace in God. We can actually live without strain, without discord, without fear, because Christ gives rest and peace of heart and mind and soul.

Chapter Four

THE NATURAL WORLD

(Genesis 1-2)

Many people have wondered about the location of the
Garden of Eden. Apparently the exact location is not known.
There are no landscape features pinpointed in the Genesis
account. There are no traditions on this subject, but the
geographical boundaries and a description of the location
of the Garden of Eden are recorded in the second chapter
of Genesis. The words are carefully chosen and one should
not doubt their reality.

> And a river went out of Eden to water the garden; and
> from thence it was parted, and became into four heads. The
> name of the first is Pison: that is it which compasseth the
> whole land of Havilah, where there is gold; And the gold
> of that land is good: there is bdellium and the onyx stone.
> And the name of the second river is Gihon: the same is it
> that compasseth the whole land of Ethiopia. And the name
> of the third river is Hiddekel: that is it which goeth toward
> the east of Assyria. And the fourth river is Euphrates
> (2:10-14).

The first three rivers are obscure and unknown to us, but
the river Euphrates continues until this day. This is the
main river in the Mesopotamian Valley and so it is generally
accepted that this in all probability was the location of the
Garden of Eden.

Apparently this garden was prepared for man. Here is
seen God's providence and care for man. Man was going to
need the fruit of the garden. But God gave him much more.
He gave him all the benefits of nature. Since man must
breathe air that contains oxygen, God provided such air.

Since man must have water to drink, by the very nature of his physical constitution, God provided water. Since man must have food to eat, so that his body might be nourished and continue its existence, God provided the food. Persons who ignore the Bible account of the creation seem to prefer to think that savage, unlearned, ignorant man took the barren raw world and started working with it, taming the wilds of this earth and the universe. But this is not the way the Bible records it. God arranged to provide the proper environment for man's continued well-being and happiness. So it is written that "God planted a garden" and this is the first great truth in this portion of the Bible. The second great truth is that God put the man whom He had formed into the garden, where he would find everything he needed. Many details are omitted, but there is one clear-cut impression: the garden was not man's discovery. He did not chance to find this and that, and then assemble things to put them together. The garden was not man's production. Man was not that wise or that able. The truth of the matter is that God provided the Garden of Eden for man.

Even to this day it is so easy for natural man to be filled with his own importance and with pride. He is tempted to think he can control his own destiny. On every side can be seen the chaos man has caused by his actions in his sinful nature. But in the beginning it was not so. God supplied every need of man. And even to this day God provides for His own. He will supply every need of His people.

The third great truth to be seen here is that God did not put man into the garden to live in idleness. "And the Lord God took the man, and put him into the garden of Eden to dress it and to keep it" (2:15). God placed before man the elements needed for his continued existence, but man would be involved in the process of bringing to pass the desired results. Note how this works. God provides the elements in their original unready form, and puts them into the hands of man with all their tremendous potential. God gives them to man for him to develop and use, but He does not force them upon man.

Even so God provides promises for our blessing. We do not find these promises in nature, nor in the planets, nor in the wooded hills, nor in running streams. His promises, which are "forever settled in the heavens," are found in the Scriptures. If the Bible is held merely as any other book, a man could own a dozen of them and not receive faith to believe the promises of God. But if the Bible is taken as His inspired Word, it becomes "food" for the soul. Just as I need food for my body, so I need food for my soul. If a man were dying of starvation and someone were to ask him: "Have you eaten?" how foolish it would be if he answered: "Yes, I had a meal three or four weeks ago!" It is well-known that bodies cannot live without food. If a man refuses to eat, he will die. Even so the soul will perish without the sustaining faith which comes by reading the Word of God.

The church on the corner will not benefit my faith unless I attend the worship services. Paul wrote to the Thessalonians, "If any man will not work, neither let him eat." These words can very well apply to the soul if a man does not read the Bible, if he does not study it. In this way a man can deprive his soul of the Bread of Life.

When it is written "In six days God created heaven and earth," something is revealed about the ways of God. When the Scriptures record in detail what happened on each day, it is obvious that creation was not a haphazard affair. It did not occur by any chance event, but by logical, orderly, related processes. In recent generations there has been much scientific research made which identifies the interrelationship between natural things and sets up an order in which the natural phenomena depend on each other. This can be seen very simply by noting the grass in the field. Grass is something a rabbit will eat and the rabbit is something a wolf will eat. In this way one species depends on another.

There is actually a balance in this ecology of nature. Grass in the field is eaten by cattle, man kills the cattle and eats the beef. While man does not eat grass, yet the food values that are in the grass come to him in the beef he eats. In checking through the order of what took place in the six days of creation, we find ten or more relationships sketched there. For instance, the land appeared before the grass, and the grass appeared before the arrival of the animals, and the animals appeared before man, who would use them for food. This order in Genesis fits modern scientific data perfectly.

Although the Bible is not a textbook on science, wherever it touches upon the various sciences it is accurate in every detail. In the days of Greek mythology men had their own ideas about the origin of man. One myth tells of a man going out at night and seeding dragon seeds in the ground, and the next morning soldiers fully armed for war came out of the ground. There is nothing so fantastic in Genesis. Another myth tells that Zeus, the greatest God of the pagans, had a terrific headache for several days, after which his head split open and Athena stepped out fully armed. There is nothing so grotesque to be found in the Bible, although it was written during the times when grotesque and fantastic ideas were the beliefs of the day. In ancient times there was another belief among some pagans that everything was created from water. Others would insist that everything came from fire. Some of these pagan theories could be called "evolution," because they all seem to hold that more complex forms developed from less complex forms by natural processes.

When in the days of my unbelief I first heard of the theory of evolution while in high school, I was much attracted to it because the idea of evolution appeals to people who do not believe in God. Believing in God leads to responsibility for our actions to Him who is supreme, and I was glad to think there might be reason not to feel responsible. But I dropped this theory before I became a Christian because there was no evidence to substantiate it. By the way, I can tell you that I have kept my eyes and ears open all these many years without noticing a single bit of proof or shred of evidence to support this theory coming to light. When I was studying for my doctorate in one of the great universities in the East, it became known in my department that I believed the Bible to be true. Fellow graduate students and professors were sure that I must be foolish. They certainly gave me no deferential treatment because I was an ordained minister. At one time my professor challenged me for the sake of class discussion to ask one question about this theory of evolution. I raised the same question I had brought up in high school. I said, "If this is a scientific fact about the origin of various forms of life, give me one, just one, illustration." This took place in the presence of one hundred and seventy-five graduate students, each of them working for a master's degree or a doctorate. Among these scientifically trained people, not one could produce such an illustration. I have found it is not possible on the basis of any evidence available. The whole issue of the validity of this theory can be handled by asking "Can you produce one case in point as evidence?"

In the Book of Genesis there is a guide to follow. It has been mentioned above. It has been pointed out that in the first fifteen verses the words "after its kind" and "after their kind" occur ten times. This is to say simply that when barley seeds are planted, men harvest barley. When men plant wheat seeds, men harvest a wheat crop. Apple trees will produce apples, and so on. The important fact this observation points out is the consistency of the natural creation. Actually there could be no science of any kind were it otherwise. If salt did not remain salt, if iron did not remain iron, if silver did not remain silver, and so on, there could be no basis for science. There may be combinations of various things, but each element must have consistency and continuity. Oxygen remains oxygen, and carbon is always carbon.

It is important to note the meaning of such facts. The consistency of natural phenomena is a function of the "righteousness of the Creator." It is God who keeps things as they are. In the New Testament we read that in Jesus Christ "all things consist." This is to say that they "hold together," because God is faithful and true. His care extends to every living creature. God not only prepared the Garden of Eden for man—He also provided for living creatures and for the plants. Everything man needed to sow and to harvest was there and awaited his use, according to God's wisdom and God's plan. God made all things and so we can rejoice when we join other Christians who confidently affirm, "I believe in God the Father, Almighty, Maker of heaven and earth."

Chapter Five

THE NATURE OF MAN

(Genesis 2)

Genesis 1:28 records how man was given his first assignment. He was to subdue the earth, which would mean that he should manage it. He was to make it serve his purposes. This provides the basis for all industry wherein men busy themselves one way or another to handle and to utilize the things that are in the natural creation. It is the ground for all science which seeks to know the earth, to control what is discovered and use it for whatever purpose man has in mind. The record goes on to say that man is to "have dominion over the fish of the sea, and the fowl of the air, and over every living thing that moveth upon the earth." This design that man should be in control can lead to a common error on the part of man.

The Bible records that man sinned, and so he did not carry out what God had in mind for him. In his own wayward, foolish sinfulness man followed his own ideas. Here it should be noted that whenever man treats other men as inanimate objects or as animals in trying to subdue them, trouble is certain to follow. When a man treats his fellow man as a thing, he violates the actual plan of God. Such procedure can cause only violent reaction because men will fight to the death not to be so dominated.

The one place where dominion can be well applied is to "self." Subduing one's own natural desires and having dominion over one's own willful, erring human nature leads to something very important. Before starting to subdue the earth or other men, a man must start with himself. I can start right in with the two hundred pounds of the dust of the earth which represents me. To bring my will under control, to gain dominion over my own natural tendencies is a matter of self-discipline. This is tremendously important. The Bible says that he who has mastery over his own spirit is "greater than he who taketh a city."

Genesis 2:7 records, "The Lord God formed man of the dust of the ground." The Hebrew word *formed* is not "make" or "create" but "build" or "fashion." The Lord God fashioned or formed man out of the dust of the ground, breathed into his nostrils the breath of life, and He put him into the garden He had planted. In the midst of the garden was one tree whose fruit was forbidden to Adam. This involves a very important principle. For the present let us call it the "separated portion." We do not know altogether why the tree was called the "tree of knowledge of good and evil," but there are some features about it that we need to notice. First we see that the tree was within the reach of man. He could lay his hands on it. Next we read that the fruit was attractive. The commandment given to man concerning this tree was without explanation, but it contained a warning. It was also a challenge to man's self-control. All the fruit of the garden was within man's reach, and he could have and enjoy everything, except the forbidden fruit. It was as though God said: "Everything is there within your reach, but you cannot have everything." In order to be a person of moral stature and uprightness, a man must be able to subdue his own willfullness and control his own desires. He must be able to say "no" to himself.

In Genesis 2:18 are these amazing and profound words: "It is not good that the man should be alone." This flat, dogmatic statement is true about all mankind anywhere, everywhere. History proves it. Biography shows it. Psychology and sociology recognize it. It is true at all levels that it is not good that man should be alone. In our day and time we refer to this as the social nature of man. And it is true that for human beings to be normal and natural, they need to be with other human beings.

Such social interaction is the origin of all human values. For those who may doubt this statement, let me illustrate. Let me ask, Is money valuable? If someone were to be stranded on a desert island all alone and starving, but with a pocketful of money, would money help him? Now, we all accept the fact that the only reason money is valuable is because it will buy for us the things we need. Every single thing we count as important is only so because of other people.

Hermits who live alone become peculiar in their thinking and in their way of life. Even a family member who withdraws himself from the family circle will become strange in his ways. Believe me, for us to live a normal, balanced life, to get the most out of life, we need to be with people. Relationships between people are important. Relationship between man and God is vital. Any estrangement or alienation from God results in a tragic isolation.

In the second part of Genesis 2:18 we read, "I will make him a help meet for him." When we put the words *help* and *meet* together, we miss so much. When we break them apart we find them meaningful. A "helper meet" for him. "Meet for him" is an old English way of saying "equal to." So actually when we say "help meet," this means much more than a companion. It refers to someone who can and will help another and who is equal to the other person. This brings to our mind a very important thing about the nature of mankind. Fellowship, in order to be important, must be with an equal. This, by the way, explains a good deal of the distress of many people. When we are so absorbed with self that we are, in our own estimation, above others, we will find no common meeting ground with others. We might as well go off by ourselves; and this is not good, and can only lead to an imbalance of our personality.

The idea of a helper originated with God. Man does not always know that he needs a helper equal to him. This is not the conclusion of social science. This is in God's benevolent plan for the welfare of man. Verses 19 and 20 bring something very positively to our minds. We read that God brought every living creature to Adam: "to see what he would call them . . . And Adam gave names to all cattle, and to the fowl of the air, and to every beast of the field." What an amazing feat! This certainly shows the intellect of man as he came from the hand of God.

The closing words of Genesis 2:20 are: "There was not found a help meet for him." As a boy on the farm I had some dogs that I remember to this day. I really appreciated and loved these pets. The same is true of the horses. One can get to know horses like one knows people, and they too can respond to us. But such animals can never fill human need or take the place of human companionship and communion.

Genesis 2:21-23 tells of the creation of woman. "The Lord God caused a deep sleep to fall upon Adam, and he slept: and he took one of his ribs (the Hebrew reads, "He took a piece of his side"), and closed up the flesh instead thereof; And the rib, which the Lord God had taken from man, made he a woman, and brought her unto the man." This is certainly a strange and amazing record. I am not going to claim that I can explain the details. However, I am sure of one thing: no animal was taken and improved and improved until it evolved into a help meet for man. The procedure of creating woman may be obscure to us, but the implications are plain. Woman is from the side of man. It has been said that she did not come from his head so as to dominate him, but rather she was taken from his side, that she might walk beside him. In marriage these two become one.

This is the origin of that concept of unity and equality which has been abused by many so-called religions. A great many people in this world belong to a certain religion in which a woman is considered a lower form of life. As a matter of fact, in that particular society man's food is considered defiled and unfit to eat if the shadow of a woman falls upon it. You may think this is strange and fantastic, but it is nevertheless true. Even civilized, intelligent men are capable of cruelty to their wives. Many people consider that the emancipation of women is a very recent thing, but in reality, in the beginning God created them equal. Woman is not to help man as a slave or a beast of burden, or by being merely a convenience. When a man recognizes the woman as his equal, he will be helped more by her aid than if he did not so recognize her. As far as a woman is concerned she will find her satisfaction and the normal fulfillment of her nature in sharing in her man's achievements: in his work and in his success. She is at her best when she supports him and shares with him. As we read in Genesis, woman was to be man's mainstay. A culture or a religion or a man who degrades woman is self-degrading. The original pattern and plan of God is still in effect even though in many cases sin has spoiled it. We read in His Word that a man will forsake all others and cleave unto his wife. There is no question about this; the Bible places woman beside man as his equal.

Chapter Six

THE FALL OF MAN

(Genesis 3)

The first two chapters of Genesis record the existence of no disturbing element. This is not the situation in our world today. It is popular on the part of some people to claim that disruptive factors are caused by ignorance and weakness. On this basis they urge education upon man. They try to inspire ambition for higher goals and better performance by assuming that mankind is capable of living successfully by itself. But the Bible does not leave matters there. It teaches that "our adversary, the devil as a roaring lion, walketh about, seeking whom he may devour." The devil is also called "Satan" and sometimes is referred to as "that old serpent." Modern teaching denies the existence of the devil, claiming that this is a figment of the imagination. No one can deny that there is trouble and disaster and calamity in this world. Some people dare to blame God for such evil, but the Bible speaks of "your adversary the devil."

In chapter 3 of the Book of Genesis, we read of the appearance of the serpent in the garden.

Now the serpent was more subtil than any beast of the field which the Lord God had made. And he said unto the woman, Yea, hath God said, Ye shall not eat of every tree of the garden? And the woman said unto the serpent, We may eat of the fruit of ,the trees of the garden: But of the fruit of the tree which is in the midst of the garden, God hath said, Ye shall not eat of it, neither shall ye touch it, lest ye die. And the serpent said unto the woman, Ye shall not surely die: For God doth know that in the day ye eat thereof, then your eyes shall be opened, and ye shall be as gods, knowing good and evil. And when the woman saw that the tree was good for food, and that it was pleasant to the eyes, and a tree to be desired to make one wise, she took of the fruit thereof, and did eat, and gave also unto her husband with her; and he did eat. And the eyes of them both were opened, and they knew that they were naked. (3:1-7a).

Let us look a little bit more closely at these words which are so familiar to us. When we read "the serpent was more subtil," no one knows for certain what these words mean. Some translators say that they suggest "more beautiful, more attractive, more clever, and more cunning." This being we have just described is called "the serpent" in the Book of Genesis. In the Book of Revelation we read these words: "the great dragon was cast out; that old serpent, called the devil and Satan, which deceiveth the whole world." And there we have it in a nutshell: "which deceiveth the whole world."

When we consider Satan as a being we ask ourselves the question: "What do we know about him?" We need not limit ourselves to this third chapter of Genesis, but may search through the Bible for this information. In the first place we find that he was created. He is a creature. That means that he was not intended to be eternal. Why did God make Satan? I do not know. Someone will say, "Then He should not have made him." This we can never say. Just because we cannot understand something, this does not make it wrong. We can trust God implicitly, and without reservation. We know He makes no mistakes. Not only is the reality of Satan true, but we are told that he is a spirit; he does not have a body such as we have.

All angels who are also created beings do not have bodies such as we have. This is true of both evil spirits and good spirits. Even the Holy Spirit of God does not have a body like ours, but He is a person. We are commonly filled with the idea that a person must have a head and arms and legs and a body. This is not true. To be a person requires only a capacity of thought and of feeling and of will. By the way, while we are thinking in this area, we discover that not only is Satan named, but Michael the archangel is also named. Gabriel, who came to Mary and announced that she would bear the Holy Son of God, is spoken of a number of times in the Bible. In fact he is the same angel who announced the coming of John the Baptist.

Many Bible teachers feel that Lucifer, spoken of in the fourteenth chapter of Isaiah, refers to Satan. This could be true, but the Bible does not so specify. There are other things that the Bible tells us of Satan. He is a liar and the father of lies. The truth is not in him. He is a murderer who seeks to destroy. He is malicious: he actually means to do us harm. But Satan has certain limitations. He is not omniscient, he does not know everything. Satan is not omnipotent, he cannot do everything. He can only move within God's permissive will. While we think of this, let us remember that Jesus of Nazareth faced Satan and was victorious. Paul, writing to the Corinthians, warns them that Satan may come transformed as an angel of light. Peter speaks of him as going about as a roaring lion, seeking whom he may devour. In other words, the Bible warns us about Satan. Here is a little couplet which I like very much: "Satan trembles when he sees, the weakest saint upon his knees." We do not have to be afraid of Satan when we are "in the Lord." But we certainly are no match for him person to person.

As we read on in chapter 3 we find a description of the course of sin. Being tempted is not an indication that we are sinning. Temptation is not sin. In this chapter we are brought face to face with the beginning of sin with all its terrible consequences. We should notice that nothing foreign or alien was injected into the situation. Sin occurred right where man was living, when he misused the very situation that was given to him to bless him. When man was created in the image of God, this included his consciousness of himself as a person with a freedom of choice. This is true today. I can choose whether to go to the right or left. I can choose whether to open the Bible and read it, or whether to leave it closed. I can pray, or I cannot pray. I am free to choose.

God gave man everything that would promote his well-being, but when God said, "This is forbidden, this you cannot have," man was to obey. Someone may say, "I do not like that idea." We should remember that we did not create this world. We do not keep it or control it. Obedience to God is not a forced or an automatic thing. It must be a conscious, willing choice. For this, man must be free. Here we have a clue as to what was involved in making man free to choose. All obedient response given to God must be freely offered.

It has been noted that Satan is a malicious murderer who wants to destroy what God has made. He is an adversary who is both cunning and shrewd, but God has set bounds beyond which he cannot go. When we put our trust and faith in the Lord Jesus Christ, we need not be afraid of him at all. There is safety in the Lord. The Israelites were safe in their homes when the angel of death passed through the land, because the blood of the lamb was over their doors. Noah was safe in the ark when the floods came upon the earth. So we who believe and trust in Christ are safe in Him.

Satan was too cunning to come up to Eve and ask her to disobey God. Eve might not have done that. But Satan raised a question about what God had said. He did not contradict God. He did not ignore the Word of God. He just questioned it and appealed to her judgment. This is a snare into which it is easy to fall even today. When man stops to think about what God had said, and tries to evaluate it, it is as though he attempted to judge God's words. Eve fell into the net the devil had prepared because the devil flattered her.

This story of "the fall" has a classic format. It happens that way over and over again when temptation comes along. Satan is a liar, but he is much too shrewd to lie openly. In this case he just called attention to something that was pleasant and attractive, and he omitted telling Eve of the tragic consequences which could follow. I am reminded of the days when a salesman would bring a new car to my home to show it. First came the looking at it, then the driving around the block. Nothing wrong with that; that was a pleasure. The salesman never said a thing about the fact that all this was going to cost more than I wanted to pay. This was the way to get a decision. Satan works in the same way. He came and drew attention to the forbidden fruit which was pleasant to the eye, and a fruit to be desired to make one wise. Satan knew that Adam and Eve would be vulnerable to judgment and death if they ate the fruit, and this is the very thing that he had planned and schemed to accomplish.

Chapter Seven

THE NATURE OF SIN

(Genesis 3)

The third chapter of Genesis records the devious way in which Satan approached Eve and tempted her to sin. In 1 John 2:16 there is described a sort of pattern which indicates the three areas in which human beings are tempted. These areas include "the lust of the flesh, and the lust of the eyes, and the pride of life." In the case of Adam and Eve in the garden "the lust of the flesh" can be seen when it is written that the fruit of the tree was "good for food." That is to say, it would satisfy appetite. It would feel good to eat it. "The lust of the eyes" in imagination can be seen in the words "pleasant to the eyes." "The pride of life" as vanity was aroused when the forbidden fruit promised "to make them wise." All of this points to a yearning to promote self. By subtle flattery Satan appealed to the woman's own interpretation of the words God had spoken to Adam. When Eve felt free to make a decision different from the directive given by God, she made a great mistake. God had said, "No. Do not eat thereof." When Eve began to think that the forbidden fruit would be good to eat, she had already disobeyed. She left herself wide open to what happened afterwards.

It will be helpful to contrast this temptation in the garden with that of Jesus of Nazareth in the desert (Matt. 4:1-11). There it is recorded that Jesus of Nazareth had fasted for forty days and was hungry when the devil approached Him. His desire for food would be in its own way the desire of the flesh. There is nothing evil about food, nothing evil about being hungry. At this time the devil proposed that Jesus of Nazareth prove His sonship by turning the stones into bread. He answered Satan with the Word of God: "It is written, Man shall not live by bread alone." Satan then took Him on a pinnacle of the temple and said, "If thou be the Son of God, cast thyself down: for it is written, He shall give his angels charge concerning thee: and in their hands they shall bear thee up, lest at any time thou dash thy foot against a stone." But He answered Satan with these words: "It is written again, Thou shalt not tempt the Lord thy God." Then the devil took Him up into a high mountain and showed Him all the kingdoms of the world and offered them to Him. Jesus of Nazareth said, "It is written, Thou shalt worship the Lord thy God, and him only shalt thou serve." Thus it is recorded that in each instance Jesus of Nazareth turned to the Word of God for His guidance. For Him it was all settled because He came into this world to do the will of His heavenly Father. And right here where Adam was weak, Jesus of Nazareth was strong.

Why is it that in the strain of living one Christian is strong and another is weak, when both are human beings? The truth may be seen in an illustration. Suppose two men go out to sea, each in his own boat. Suddenly a terrific storm approaches. Each boat has an anchor with which it can be secured to avoid being smashed on the rocks. But one man is so confident in the strength of his boat and the way in which it is built that he leaves the anchor lying in the hold of the ship. He has the anchor and he has the cable, but if he does not use what he has, his position is perilous in the face of the storm. The other man is in the same danger, but he takes his anchor and casts it into the rocks at the bottom of the sea. When that anchor holds, it holds the boat in place because it is secured to something outside itself that is solid and strong. This is just what we have in the Gospel of Jesus Christ. When I put my trust in God, my faith is like an anchor of the soul that takes hold of the infinite power of God. This is the significance of my strength.

I can hold steady and be faithful when I am anchored in Him.

This same truth can be seen in another example. Suppose there are two mothers and each of them has a sick baby. One of these mothers is confident in her own skill and her own supplies. She applies her own remedy because she is absolutely sure that she can take care of her baby. She does everything she can, but her baby dies. The other woman is not so confident about herself. She has confidence in her doctor and she brings her baby to him and follows his instructions and her baby gets well. Certainly, each mother wanted her baby to live. The first one was confident in herself. The second one had confidence in her doctor, and she obeyed him. The one that trusted herself was foolish. The one who trusted someone with superior knowledge was wise.

When Adam was tested in the garden he viewed the temptation in his own judgment and decided that the fruit would be something to accept and eat. He did not follow the commandment of God, his Creator. Jesus of Nazareth met every temptation with the Word of God. May we who desire to walk in the strength of our Savior turn to His Word in the day of our temptation to sin.

Many people do not really know what sin is. Sin is best understood when man has an awareness of God. It is when we think of the holiness of God that we become conscious of our sinfulness. If a man had no idea of God, he would have no idea of sin. Today we use the word *sin* rather loosely. We talk about sinning against society, sinning against children, and sinning against people. In the Bible we read that all sin is sinning against God. Men say "crime" is against man, but we commit "sin" against God. However, every crime and every wrongdoing violates His law.

The Bible records the occurrence of the first sin in the Garden of Eden. When God told Adam not to eat of the fruit of the tree of knowledge of good and evil He did not offer any reason for this; man was not only forbidden to eat this fruit, but he was warned of the consequences of disobedience: "In the day that thou eatest thereof thou shalt surely die." This indicates that man must not act according to his own judgment when God has spoken concerning a certain thing. Things are not right or wrong just because we judge them to be so. However, if I am asked to do something which I think is wrong, then it would be wrong for me to do it. On the basis of what is written in Genesis 3, I am to be obedient to His Word. Some people will claim that this is too elementary. They say that implicit obedience is for children. But Jesus of Nazareth taught, "Except ye be converted, and become as little children, ye shall not enter into the kingdom of heaven" (Matt. 18:3). I need not be afraid to emulate little children because this is the very way in which I can come to Him. Being childlike in faith and trust is far removed from being childish.

Many earnest hearts are burdened with a sense of shame because of certain thoughts that plague them. They have a sense of sin, because evil thoughts appear in their minds and burden their consciences. Any who are burdened about this may keep in mind that no human being can be free from evil thoughts. Evil thoughts come like the seeds of a weed that will fly through the air and fall into the garden. Anyone who has planted a garden has found plants growing in it that were not planted. The man who has a lawn will find amongst the grass weeds which he did not plant. They came in from the outside. They blew in, so to speak. The same thing that is true of the unwanted weeds in our garden is true concerning our minds.

All of us will at some time or another be troubled by thoughts that are hateful to us. In our day and time a good deal is made of thought transference. Psychology recognizes what is called "extrasensory perception," which implies that one person can become aware of what is in another person's mind. This would only emphasize what I am talking about. Isaiah the prophet said, "I am a man of unclean lips, and I dwell in the midst of a people of unclean lips." To say we live in the midst of people of unclean lips is to say unclean thoughts are in the air. At the same time it should be remembered that when it comes to temptation, nothing that I do not want tempts me, even when it comes from the outside.

Crude and vulgar thoughts may come to mind and we may promptly disown and hate them. Ugly thoughts may come to our minds at times, and certainly we would not want anyone else to know such had even crossed our minds, yet none of these thoughts need lead us to sin. All men are not alike, and the sins they are tempted to commit are different. One man may be tempted by whiskey, and the thought of it may fill him with desire. Another man may be repelled by whiskey. The very thought of it may be abhorrent to him. I happen to be one of those people who fortunately grew up in a home where people were very careful in their conduct. When I was a student in high school the idea of drinking had no appeal for me at all.

We should be very careful not to ascribe our thoughts to other people whose thinking may be very different from ours. When evil thoughts come to our minds and linger there, they may show us how sinful we are. This may be because deep down inside us we actually like them. Or it could mean that we are fascinated by them because they horrify us. In other words many things may tempt us and appeal to us and yet not be sinful.

Sin is the act which follows inclination to evil. Sin does not need to be vulgar or ugly. Sin can be clean and refined, but if it puts us outside the will of God it is sin. Had Eve only looked at the forbidden fruit and seen how pleasant and desirable it was, this would not have been wrong. Her tragic mistake was that she took it upon herself to defy the direct command of God. Her sin, which brought such terrible consequences with it, was disobedience. We will see how this disobedience marred forever their innocence, how it caused them to be driven out of the beautiful garden the Lord God had planted for their enjoyment, and how it brought havoc to all nature. However, we will also read of the way God provided to remove their sin and guilt.

Chapter Eight

THE CONSEQUENCES OF SIN

(Genesis 3)

The sin of Adam, in the form of disobedience to God, brought sin into the world. Each person living in this world is contaminated with it. God who is sovereign of the whole universe and who holds everything in His hand, is also the judge of all men. Because of this, God must deal with our sins. We are responsible human beings, and therefore it is unavoidable that we must pay the penalty of our sin. God is the judge and He must rule on our guilt. There is nothing so amazing or so remarkable or difficult about this. When we face the judge, we must first of all admit that we have done wrong. We must confess openly that we are guilty. It's a matter of calling a spade a spade, and this is basic to all the judgment of God. This does not require any action on God's part. He not only knows all about our wrongdoings and why we committed them, but He has evaluated them from the beginning. His estimation of our deeds was there all the time, and this is basic to all that follows afterward. The very act of creation makes God sovereign, and man as creature is responsible to obey Him.

It would appear that people have developed a whole set of wrong ideas around the notion of freedom. They seem to think they can do as they please. This is not true. Every time we hear of a man who has been drinking and who winds up with his car in the ditch, we can be sure that he has found out the consequences of his action. When a man feels that he can choose as he pleases, he may choose blindly without weighing the consequences. As a result he may find that he has run into a stone wall. When a man is willful he violates the constitution of the creation. God does not tolerate this. God made man in such a way that he should obey God's law and His will. When man disobeyed God he automatically came under the condemnation of God. At the very time that man sinned, God knew and evaluated the sin and fixed the penalty for it.

To disobey the will of God is sin, and in every man there is an inner awareness that when he disobeys God he will suffer for it. "The soul that sinneth, it shall die." Judgment is implicit in the very nature of things. There is a sense in which judgment is a good deal like darkness. Darkness is always implicit. In other words it is absolute. The moment the light is put out, the room is dark. The darkness is right there; and it is the inevitable consequence of the absence of light. We did not have to pump anything into the room to make it dark. So it is with death. When a person dies we recognize that death is the absence of life. Life is a positive factor, and when life is gone, death is there. It follows automatically even the way darkness follows the absence of light. This is the way it is with judgment. When a man does wrong, obedience moves out and judgment moves in. That's all there is to it. The whole concept that God punishes the culprit in vengeance is erroneous. The sinner brings judgment upon himself.

In Genesis 3:9 we have the record of the famous question: "Where art thou?" This was not asked for information. God knew what Adam had done and where he was. This question was asked to help Adam. "Where art thou?" could be put in this way: "Now that you have done what you have done, where did it get you?" Adam's conscience needed to be aroused that he might be ready to confess his sin. God's judgment was settled all the time, but Adam did not know this. He might have thought that he could escape notice. So he needed to hear this question, "Where has your disobedience brought you?"

Actually Adam was already a changed man. It is written, "The eyes of them both were opened, and they knew that they were naked; and they sewed fig leaves together, and made themselves aprons." Apparently they already had the sickening realization which follows wrongdoing. Then they tried by their own inadequate efforts to make themselves acceptable. This did not work, and so they realized their own helplessness. When God said, "Who told thee that thou wast naked? Hast thou eaten of the tree?" He wanted to focus Adam's attention on his wrongdoing. It is only when man will recognize that God's judgment follows directly upon his sin, that he realizes his desperate need for grace and the mercy of God. It is when I become aware of the fact that I am responsible for my sins, and know that judgment awaits me, that I am ready to cry out, "Woe is me, I am undone."

All who feel their lost condition may know there is a way of escape which God Himself has prepared. Human beings in themselves are so prone to blame others for their mistakes. They always seek for reasons behind their trouble and suffering. It is true that men live in a world which is full of trouble. Pain and sorrow are universal. Many people ascribe distress to ignorance, and say that education is the answer to this world's ills. Some say that distress is caused by aggression. They say we must stop the aggressors. Some say that distress is caused by pride and jealousy and selfishness. In all of this there is one common underlying idea; everyone agrees on one point: there is something wrong, and if this wrong is righted, all will be well.

The Bible points out that it is man who is at fault, rather than his circumstances or his environment or other people who live around him. Man was created in the image of God as a free moral agent. Adam was given the opportunity to lead a sinless life in a world where pain and death, trouble and strife were unknown. When Adam chose to sin, he involved all who would be born after him in sin. In Adam all men are sinful. Here is an aspect of human nature that has profound implications. In the Book of Hebrews we read of Abraham paying tithes to Melchizedec, the king of Salem. The writer of the Book of Hebrews goes on to say that "in Abraham," his descendants shared in this act, in the same way as all the descendants of Adam share in his sinful nature. This is sometimes called the federal headship of Adam. In other words, Adam had in himself all mankind.

The importance of this truth is that in this same way all believers are in Jesus Christ. Just as all men were in Adam, so all believers are in Christ. Just as in the fall of Adam all men fell, the amazing truth is that because Christ lived righteously, all believers are lifted unto righteousness.

> Wherefore, as by one man sin entered into the world, and death by sin; and so death passed upon all men, for that all have sinned: (For until the law sin was in the world: but sin is not imputed when there is no law. Nevertheless death reigned from Adam to Moses, even over them that had not sinned after the similitude of Adam's transgression, who is the figure of him that was to come. But not as the offence, so also is the free gift. For if through the offence of one many be dead, much more the grace of God, and the gift by grace, which is by one man, Jesus Christ, hath abounded unto many. And not as it was by one that sinned, so is the gift: for the judgment was by one to condemnation, but the free gift is of many offences unto justification. For if by one man's offence death reigned by one; much more they which receive abundance of grace and of the gift of righteousness shall reign in life by one, Jesus Christ.) Therefore as by the offence of one judgment came upon all men to condemnation; even so by the righteousness of one the free gift came upon all men unto justification of life. For as by one man's disobedience many were made sinners, so by the obedience of one shall many be made righteous (Rom. 5:12-19).

The message of this passage of Scripture is plain. Just as sin and death came by Adam, so grace and life came by Christ. The relationship of Adam to the rest of mankind is easy enough to understand because of biological connection: it is obvious all men came from Adam. But the relationship of Christ to all believers is a spiritual connection which escapes our sight. It is the work of the Holy Spirit. We cannot see it, but it is there. It is true. It is an astonishing and wonderful truth that grace abounds much more than sin ever could.

In chapter 3 of Genesis the dire consequences of Adam's

sin are recorded. It is a short chapter simply written which contains the profound truth that while the practical details may differ in regard to where and how men live, the general aspects of sin are always present.

This chapter shows the consequences of Adam's fall. First of all there was the loss of innocence. After Adam and Eve had eaten of the forbidden fruit, their eyes were opened and they knew that they were naked. Innocence, which had clothed them as a garment, was gone. Then is the record of Adam's and Eve's futile attempts to cover up. They made themselves aprons of fig leaves and hid themselves from the presence of God. But they were called on to give a reason for what they had done, because they were responsible for their actions. Even so human beings are always responsible, not only for what they do, but also for what they hear and follow. Men are responsible for the guidance they follow.

Another consequence of the fall is enmity between the serpent and the seed of the woman. In the words "the seed of the woman," there is something unique and strange. It would be a normal thing to speak of the "seed of a man," so it is accepted by Bible students that "the seed of a woman" actually predicts the virgin birth of Jesus Christ of Nazareth. This is seen as the first prophecy that Christ in His life and death and resurrection would triumph over Satan.

As a further consequence of the fall, woman was destined to suffer pain and sorrow. Generally speaking, in many cultures woman is helpless and often abused. Also since the fall man must do his work under difficulties. Originally Adam was to tend the beautiful Garden of Eden, but now outside of the garden thorns and thistles would make his labor hard.

> Thorns also and thistles shall it bring forth to thee; and thou shalt eat the herb of the field; In the sweat of thy face shalt thou eat bread, till thou return unto the ground; for out of it wast thou taken: for dust thou art, and unto dust shalt thou return (Gen. 3:18-19).

The most shattering and tragic consequence of man's fall

was his alienation from God. The Lord God sent him forth from the Garden of Eden to till the soil from whence he was created.

> So he drove out the man; and he placed at the east of the garden of Eden Cherubims, and a flaming sword which turned every way, to keep the way of the tree of life (3:24).

Thus man was alienated from his Creator and God, and so must find some way to be reconciled to Him that he may be blessed. Thank God that He Himself in love and mercy sent the Gospel of Jesus Christ into this condemned world. God is calling to men everywhere, "Be ye reconciled to God" through the complete atonement of Jesus Christ on Calvary, who paid for our sins by dying for them. "Whosoever will may come."

Chapter Nine

CAIN AND ABEL

(Genesis 4)

It will be helpful to review the great truths revealed in the first three chapters of Genesis. Here is the record of God's creation of the heavens and the earth. Here is described the nature of man who was created in the image of God, and was told to subdue the earth and have dominion over all living creatures. Man was created with freedom of choice and a responsibility to obey God. The record tells how man was tempted and how he yielded to temptation and fell, incurring the judgment of God. There is also recorded that as a consequence of his sin, man was shut out of the garden and was alienated from God.

And now is reported the most remarkable truth in all creation. There is nothing so wonderful in all this universe as the grace of God toward fallen man. We can understand that God is holy. We can accept that He is Judge. That He will condemn sin stands to reason. All of this we could accept. Man is separated from God because of his disobedience, alienated because of his sinfulness, and doomed to die. In other words, man is lost and hopeless. He faces utter destruction. Then is revealed this wonderful truth that God is compassionate and pities man. The grace of God, the undeserved kindness and favor of God toward man, is more than can ever be understood. God paid an unspeakable price to save sinful man. Paul wrote these words, "God commendeth His love toward us, in that while we were yet sinners, Christ died for the ungodly."

To appreciate the grace of God we must recognize and realize that man had no claim on the mercy of God. There was no reason why God should show him mercy. When Adam and Eve sinned and as a result knew that they were naked, they tried unsuccessfully to cover themselves, and then hid from the presence of God. But God did not leave them to themselves in their guilt. He came looking for them, calling them to Himself. Even though they had sinned, God did not leave them to the consequences of their wrongdoing. Sinful men do not turn to God, any more than a lawbreaker turns to a judge. When a person has done wrong he does not hunt a policeman, but he runs and hides. The call of God to Adam was personal and specific. So the Lord calls to each person, to each one of us personally and specifically, in order that we may realize and recognize our need. In nature God will make the sun shine and the rain fall; He will cause the grass to grow, and the flowers to bloom, and the fruit to form and ripen. God will do all this regardless of whether or not man understands His ways in nature. But when it comes to the salvation of man, when God stoops down to save the sinner instead of condemning him, God wants man to be aware of his great need. At the same time the sinner is to be aware of the boundless love of God which saves all who come to Him in faith.

I recall that when I first came to know the Gospel, I thought that one sin should not convict a person. An old farmer, with whom I discussed my feelings, asked me, "How many men would you have to kill to become a murderer? If you let a hundred men live, this will not help you or let you off if you had killed one." So it is! Unless God intervenes in grace and mercy, we must pay the penalty for our sin. It is when we, in repentance and humility, accept God's grace which is in Christ Jesus that we know the meaning of the words, "the joy of His salvation." Some people seem to think that if they are ever saved by the grace of God they will then be perfect. Such thinking can only lead to disappointment and frustration. When we are saved by trusting God and accepting Christ Jesus as our Redeemer, we do not become angels. That is not the way it goes. But we should realize that God, by being gracious and merciful, does not condone sin. "God is angry with the wicked every day." Then why and under what circumstances does God perform His work of salvation? There is but one answer: "God so loved the world, that he gave his only begotten Son, that whosoever believeth in him should not perish, but have everlasting life."

It has been noted above that in Genesis 3:15 is given an amazing prophecy of the virgin birth, and of the day when the seed of the woman would destroy the devil. Genesis 3:21 records that God made coats of skin for Adam and Eve. The preparing of these garments involved the death of some animals and foreshadows the death of the Lamb of God. Even so, by dying in our place and stead Christ provides a robe of righteousness for all believers of all time.

It is amazing that all men do not accept and rejoice in this full and free salvation, and believe His Word as it is written. Perhaps natural man is flattered when he thinks he has evolved from some form of lower life. Jesus of Nazareth believed the Old Testament implicitly. There are many proofs of the authenticity of the Bible, but if there were no other proof except that Jesus Christ believed the Bible story of creation and quoted it as true, that would be good enough for me. This is exactly where I stand. All who refuse to accept the Scriptures and to believe them as the Word of God will be held responsible and will be judged by God.

The fourth chapter of Genesis records something very distressing about the nature of man as it is revealed in the Bible. It is a common thing to speak of brotherly affection, but it is not always true in human experience that men who are brothers are kind and helpful to one another. Being blood brothers does not assure kindly affection.

> And Adam knew Eve his wife; and she conceived, and bare Cain, and said, I have gotten a man from the Lord. And she again bare his brother Abel. And Abel was a keeper of sheep, but Cain was a tiller of the ground. And in process of time it came to pass, that Cain brought of the fruit of the ground an offering unto the Lord. And Abel, he also brought of the firstlings of his flock and

of the fat thereof. And the Lord had respect unto Abel and to his offering: but unto Cain and to his offering he had not respect. And Cain was very wroth, and his countenance fell (Gen. 4:1-5).

The simple truth is that it made Cain angry to see that Abel was preferred before him. Cain and Abel had the same parents. They lived in the same house and in the same environment. It is true that they had different occupations, but they lived in the same kind of situation. Both worshiped God by bringing sacrifices to Him: yet Abel and his offering were acceptable to God, whereas Cain and his offering were not acceptable to Him. I am aware that some people think the difference was in the offerings, but I am inclined to think that the difference was in the men themselves. Consider two men attending church services on any given Sunday. Both are sitting in the same church but one of them is acceptable to God, while the other may not be acceptable to Him. We know that this does not depend on how attentive they appear as they participate in the worship service. It does not depend on their intelligence or on their clothes. It does not depend on how much they give. In the sight of God it depends on what frame of mind each had when he came to worship. So it was with Cain and Abel.

In the case of Cain, the man is mentioned first, and then his offering. It will help our understanding to note a passage in the first Book of John which refers to Cain. First John 3:12 reports, "Not as Cain, who was of that wicked one, and slew his brother. And wherefore slew he him? Because his own works were evil, and his brother's righteous." It was the man himself who was being judged. Cain's feeling was that he had been unfairly treated. This reaction generated from self. He had noticed that Abel's offering was preferred, and he felt angry. This jealousy developed into hatred, and this in turn resulted in a dangerous attitude on Cain's part. "And the Lord said unto Cain, Why art thou wroth? and why is thy countenance fallen?" The Hebrew word for "thy countenance fallen" is literally translated "thy cheeks are fallen." We've seen sulky, angry people whose cheeks actually seem to be sagging. The corners of their mouths sag too. "If thou doest well, shalt thou not be accepted?" How clearly this question shows that Cain had not done well, since he was not accepted.

"If thou doest not well, sin lieth at the door." The words "sin lieth at the door" in Hebrew convey the idea of a beast crouching to spring. It is the way a tiger would be ready to pounce on a man. This is a rather dramatic way of saying, "Beware, when you are in an angry frame of mind. You are liable to do something terribly wrong." "Sin lieth at thy door. And unto thee shall be his desire, and thou shalt rule over him." This is saying that sin was lying in wait for Cain, and he would need to master it.

> And Cain talked with Abel his brother: and it came to pass, when they were in the field, that Cain rose up against Abel his brother, and slew him. And the Lord said unto Cain, Where is Abel thy brother? And he said, I know not: Am I my brother's keeper? And he said, What hast thou done? the voice of thy brother's blood crieth unto me from the ground (4:8-10).

Being in the field together was no doubt an ordinary, routine matter for these brothers. This was not anything exceptional. The setting had nothing to do with the crime itself. It was the hatred in the soul of Cain that mattered. There were no other people around who could have influenced him. There were no social entanglements as far as Cain was concerned. We see that God holds Cain personally responsible for his act. God calls him to account, "And the Lord said unto Cain, Where is Abel thy brother? And he said, I know not: Am I my brother's keeper? And he said, What hast thou done? the voice of thy brother's blood crieth unto me from the ground." God had in mercy warned Cain. He had given Cain an opportunity to do right, but Cain's jealousy led him out of line with God. It alienated him from God. How often even today people whose hearts are filled with hatred and jealousy turn away from the warning voice of their conscience! They ignore the admonition of God's Word and become involved in acts of violence from which there is no return.

Chapter Ten

THE WORLD BEFORE THE FLOOD

(Genesis 5)

Genesis in chapter 4 makes it plain that evil doing must and will be punished. Of course no parent who loves his child takes pleasure in inflicting punishment. But the fact is that children are not born with a knowledge of right and wrong. This they must learn, and here the parent can help. There are some basic principles of conduct the child must learn to respect. Parents and teachers can teach, but there must be some actual chastisement of the wrong and some open approval of the right to confirm the learning process.

Many of the commands the parent gives are actually for the child's own welfare, but this he may not recognize. Thus it may be simply a matter of punishing disobedience by way of training obedience to the given rules and directives. Thus a mother may spank a child for running out on the highway. This would be not only because the child has disobeyed his mother, but because of the danger involved. The child must learn to obey for his own good.

Why does a parent rebuke a child when he is impudent? Because the child is going to live with other people, and if he is allowed to be impudent at home, he will be that way with other people, and that kind of a person will not get along in the world. Why does a father discipline the boy or girl who is disobedient? Because he wants his child to grow up in such a way as to be able to get along in this world. In Hebrews 12:9-11 it is written:

Furthermore we have had fathers of our flesh which

corrected us, and we gave them reverence: shall we not much rather be in subjection unto the Father of spirits, and live? For they verily for a few days chastened us after their own pleasure; but he for our profit, that we might be partakers of his holiness. Now no chastening for the present seemeth to be joyous, but grievous: nevertheless afterward it yieldeth the peaceable fruit of righteousness unto them which are exercised thereby.

There is a difference between punishment and chastening. A rebellious, unwilling child is punished by his parent. If, however, a child really tries to please his father, makes a mistake and does wrong, the father will chasten him that he may learn thereby. The word *chasten* has in it the idea of refining, the way precious metals are refined. We may ask, "If the wrongdoer has no intention of changing his ways, why punish him?" Because swift and sure punishment will hinder and deter the wrongdoer in his further conduct.

This can be seen even in the matter of crossing the street where traffic is involved: it makes a difference if a policeman is present. His presence is enough to make us watch the crosswalk and drive more carefully. In the same way our courts and our penal institutions contribute to the measure of safety and security and peace we have in the community. We need a police force for our own protection and for the protection of our homes. Evildoers must receive just punishment.

Ezekiel 18:4 warns that "the soul that sinneth, it shall die." Adam and Eve's punishment was something they brought on themselves, but this did not make it any less terrible. We see God's grace in the covering He prepared for them. God does not reach down and take the sinner by force to punish him. Sin itself as we have seen brings judgment and punishment with it. God's grace delivers us from the consequences of His judgment. Cain's sin was not only against God. In a certain sense it was against mankind and it brought with it estrangement and isolation. In Genesis 4:12-13 it is written, "When thou tillest the ground, it shall not henceforth yield unto thee her strength; a fugitive and a vagabond shalt thou be in the earth. And Cain said unto the Lord, My punishment is greater than I can bear." Why was this punishment so terrible? We may not realize how terrible it must be to be a vagabond, homeless and friendless! Here we can see an aspect of the pangs of hell.

In penitentiaries the worst punishment meted out is not physical beatings: it is solitary confinement. No one who has not experienced such isolation will know how intolerable this can be. People have lost their minds in such a situation. Here is the awful result of hatred of other people. The consequence of destroying other people, of getting rid of other people, is to be doomed to an eternity of isolation. Some people talk carelessly about hell as if going there were a small matter; but actually we know one thing for certain: hell is a place of eternal separation from God. Since God is light and love and peace and joy and righteousness, hell will be devoid of all this. That leaves a frightening vacuum which is endless.

One thing I can say about hell is that no one needs to go there. God did not prepare hell for human beings, but for Satan and his angels. All men can be saved from hell. Christ Jesus paid for the sins of all men, so that all may be saved for heaven. Paul writes, "The love of God constraineth us, knowing the terror of the Lord, we seek to persuade men." We actually seek to win people to the Lord, with whom is abundant mercy and pardon.

When we read in the Bible that Cain left the presence of the Lord, we do not know how many years he was a homeless wanderer before he settled down in the land of Nod. We must assume that he built a home there because we read of his marriage and the birth of his first son, whom he named Enoch. When we look at the record we find that Adam lived nine hundred and thirty years and "begat sons and daughters." How many? We are not told, but we can assume that there were many sons and daughters born to Adam and Eve. Without a doubt Cain married one of the daughters of Adam and Eve.

The record shows that Cain built a city and called it after his firstborn son Enoch. After the building of this city there developed what might be called the civilization of

Cain. Special mention is made of Lamech's son Jabal, who developed ranching, whose people lived in tents and traveled around as nomads do to this day. Jabal's brother Tubal was the father of all those that handle the harp and the organ. Another brother called Tubal-cain was an instructor of every artifice in brass and iron. The sister of Tubal-cain was Naamah. So here we apparently have a whole civilization: ranching, music, and craftsmanship. But there is not one word about God in this report of the culture of the descendants of Cain.

There is no way of knowing how advanced people in those early days were. Sometime later than this, but long before the dawn of our history, the pyramids were built. They are so remarkably constructed that they are one of the wonders of the world even today. No one has ever been able to explain how these great blocks of stone could be moved into the desert plains of Egypt and built into pyramids so geometrically true. There is no clue as to how those tremendous blocks of stone were lifted without any machinery. We may conclude it definitely indicates that people living in prehistoric times had remarkable intelligence.

Another aspect in the account for which the Bible gives us no clue is the age of the early earth dwellers. Many of these lived to be hundreds of years old. We do find a statement in the Bible to the effect that after the flood, man was to live a shorter span of life. We read that Noah was a preacher of righteousness for one hundred and twenty years. Abraham, we know, lived to be one hundred and seventy-five years of age. Sarah lived one hundred and twenty-seven years, Joseph lived one hundred and ten years, and Moses lived for one hundred and twenty years. In the Psalms, man's age is spoken of as being seventy to eighty years. We may wonder why the life span was so drastically cut after the flood, but we do not find the answer in the Bible for this. We do know that in the animal kingdom there are great differences in their life spans. A dog is old at twelve to fifteen years. A horse may live to be thirty, a cow rarely lives twenty years, but an elephant can live hundreds of years. No one knows biologically why this should be the case.

Another verse that has caused much fruitless speculation is Genesis 6:2: "That the sons of God saw the daughters of men that they were fair; and they took them wives of all which they chose." It may well be that the "sons of God" refer to the sons of Seth, who was a God-fearing man, and that they married the descendants of Cain. This simple explanation is in keeping with other facts we find in the Bible on intermarriage. "There were giants in the earth in those days . . . mighty men which were of old, men of renown" (Gen. 6:4). This would imply there were men in that time of great physical prowess. But in verses 5 to 8 we read a tragic commentary on their way of life: "The wickedness of man was great . . . every imagination of the thoughts of his heart was only evil continually."

The record is plain that it grieved the heart of the Lord to see men rushing headlong to destruction because of their evil ways. The text reads "It repented the Lord." This does not mean "repent" as we would use the word referring to sinful man, but rather this word is used here to adapt the record to the understanding of man. It conveys the idea that God would not tolerate sin, but that it brings judgment and death. It is commonly true that men die sooner or later, but in the days of Noah all those living, except Noah and his family, died at one time when the flood came upon the earth. "I will destroy man whom I created from the face of the earth." Even as God who is holy must punish sin, so God who is gracious and merciful must save the just and the righteous from judgment as He did in the case of Noah.

When we look about us we see that people today are living much the same as the people who lived in Noah's day. There is an idea abroad that since God made man, He will never destroy him. How foolish such thinking is! Man is hoping desperately that the law of the harvest, "Whatsoever a man soweth that shall he also reap," is not really true. But this law is basic and inescapable. "The soul that sinneth, it shall die." To be sure, the heart of man is easily deceived, and for this reason God has made His plan very clear. In the flood He showed His ways to the whole world, to every culture, to every country. Surely no one can read the account of the Flood without realizing that the judgment of God, though long delayed, will certainly come. In judgment God destroys the ungodly, but in mercy He saves all who put their trust in Him. This great truth is manifested in the story of the Flood.

Chapter Eleven

THE FLOOD

(Genesis 6-8)

There are many references to the Flood in the New Testament in addition to the account found recorded in the Book of Genesis.

> For as in the days that were before the flood they were eating and drinking, marrying and giving in marriage, until the day that Noah entered into the ark, and knew not until the flood came, and took them all away; so shall also the coming of the Son of man be (Matt. 24:38-39).

This is a description of life as it was lived in the days of Noah. It actually describes life today. Those people who lived wicked, dissolute, godless lives were given ample warning to turn from their evil ways. Noah was a "just man and perfect in his generations" and preached to the people of his day, warning them of the judgment of God. Because "the earth was filled with violence," God spoke to Noah and told him of the destruction which He would bring upon the earth: "Behold, I, even I, do bring a flood of waters upon the earth."

God showed Noah a way of escape: "Make thee an ark of gopher wood." Not only did God warn Noah to build an ark, but He gave him all the specifications for it. No doubt Noah was mocked, ridiculed, and despised by the men of that day for building this big ship on dry land in the fear that a flood would descend upon the earth. These men lived on in their wickedness in utter disregard of God's promised judgment. This demonstrates again that just because men do not believe that God will act and do as He has spoken, this does not make a bit of difference as to what God will do. In His own time God sent the flood to destroy that generation.

This fate of unbelievers arouses sober thoughts about the future. The loose, casual views about the judgment of God which are so popular today influence so many people and lull them into a sense of false security. There are many passages of Scripture predicting the future which are variously interpreted, but all emphasize very clearly that God will not tolerate evil.

> And spared not the old world, but saved Noah the eighth person, a preacher of righteousness, bringing in the flood upon the world of the ugodly (2 Pet. 2:5).

> Knowing this first, that there shall come in the last days scoffers, walking after their own lusts, and saying, Where is the promise of his coming? for since the fathers fell asleep, all things continue as they were from the beginning of the creation. For this they willingly are ignorant of, that by the word of God the heavens were of old, and the earth standing out of the water and in the water: Whereby the world that then was, being overflowed with water, perished: But the heavens and the earth, which are now, by the same word are kept in store, reserved unto fire against the day of judgment and perdition of ungodly men (2 Pet. 3:3-7).

These words should shock men everywhere out of complacency and indifference. The Flood is the classic example of the judgment of God which will surely come. The next time that judgment comes it will be by fire.

> And Enoch also, the seventh from Adam, prophesied of these, saying, Behold, the Lord cometh with ten thousands of his saints, to execute judgment upon all, and to convince all that are ungodly among them of all their ungodly deeds which they have ungodly committed, and of all their hard speeches which ungodly sinners have spoken against him (Jude 14-15).

The record of the Flood shows that sin had become universal. "God saw that the wickedness of man was great in the earth, and that every imagination of the thoughts of his heart was only evil continually" (Gen. 6:5). This brings to our minds that the conduct and every thought of man is known to God. Nothing is hid from Him. Yet here it is recorded that hand in hand with God's judgment on evil His mercy went out to Noah, who "walked with God." Just as Noah entered the ark to escape the flood, so men today may flee for safety to Christ Jesus, who is their Ark of Safety. Noah obeyed God in preparing the ark as he was commanded. So I am to find my Ark of Safety by studying and believing God's infallible and inspired Word. I am to believe and trust in God, as He has set forth His promises in His Word. How wonderful to read that "whosoever believeth in Him shall never perish, but have everlasting life!" Thus it is man himself who decides his eternal destiny by accepting or rejecting the mercy of God.

The story of Noah reveals a message that is hopeful for the world today. Noah lived at a time when all men were given over to being exceedingly sinful, when their every thought was wicked and evil. What happened to him shows that even if sin abounds in our day, those who believe God's Word can find grace in the eyes of the Lord. Even if everyone else around me is an unbeliever, I can yet believe in God and be saved. I can turn to Him and He will receive me.

When the waters of the flood had subsided, Noah and his family came out of the ark. The first thing he did was to build an altar to worship God. A new start is very important, and after that I need a new way of life. I need more than just another chance tomorrow; I need another heart. I need to think differently. A new life must be centered around the altar, the place of worship, where I look up to God and remember that my life is in His hands and that I am responsible to Him. God is merciful and full of compassion, and I am privileged to walk with God and live in blessing as Noah did.

Noah sacrificed burnt offerings upon the altar, "of every clean beast, and of every clean fowl." The Lord accepted the sacrifice of Noah and made a promise to him.

> And I will establish my covenant with you; neither shall
> all flesh be cut off any more by the waters of a flood;
> neither shall there any more be a flood to destroy the
> earth (Gen. 9:11).

The record shows that God blessed Noah and his sons. Noah
received the same blessing Adam had been given, but God
gave him more than that.

In this covenant with Noah there is a new element. Man
is to be responsible to control his fellow man that he may
protect the innocent. In the course of time some men would
take advantage of and hurt others. The responsibility for
restraining all such aggressors was now put into the hands
of men. The following statement is classic and is basic to
all real government of men.

> Whoso sheddeth man's blood, by man shall his blood be
> shed: for in the image of God made he man (9:6).

Life was not to be destroyed at any man's pleasure. Man
was to counter force with force and thus restrain evildoers.
When an aggressor threatens the life of an innocent person,
other men are to stop him. If he takes the life of an innocent person, other men are to take his life. This is God's
directive and it is the basis for capital punishment.

In this covenant there is also the basis for war. It is right
to go to war to protect the innocent. God sealed His covenant with Noah in these words:

> And it shall come to pass, when I bring a cloud over the
> earth, that the bow shall be seen in the cloud: And I
> will remember my covenant, which is between me and
> you and every living creature of all flesh; and the waters
> shall no more become a flood to destroy all flesh. And
> the bow shall be in the cloud; and I will look upon it,
> that I may remember the everlasting covenant between
> God and every living creature of all flesh that is upon the
> earth. And God said unto Noah, This is the token of the
> covenant, which I have established between me and all
> flesh that is upon the earth (9:14-17).

As long as the rainbow appears in the heavens it is a
sign that there will never be another flood which will destroy the earth. The Bible does teach that one day the earth

will be judged by fire (2 Pet. 3:7), but never again by
water.

> And Noah began to be an husbandman, and he planted
> a vineyard: And he drank of the wine, and was drunken;
> and he was uncovered within his tent. And Ham, the
> father of Canaan, saw the nakedness of his father, and
> told his two brethren without. And Shem and Japheth
> took a garment, and laid it upon both their shoulders, and
> went backward, and covered the nakedness of their
> father; and their faces were backward, and they saw not
> their father's nakedness. And Noah awoke from his wine,
> and knew what his younger son had done unto him. And
> he said, Cursed be Canaan; a servant of servants shall he
> be unto his brethren. And he said, Blessed be the Lord
> God of Shem; and Canaan shall be his servant. God shall
> enlarge Japheth, and he shall dwell in the tents of Shem;
> and Canaan shall be his servant (Gen. 9:20-27).

This story contains a very profound truth. It shows that
lack of respect is a major blemish. Also it reveals that lack
of charity is a fundamental weakness. Both of these faults
were in Ham. He saw his father in an embarrassing condition. Some may take exception to this story because it reports that Noah was "drunken" while he was asleep. This
is actually not of any importance to the truth to be observed
here. Ham saw his father in this situation and went out and
told his brothers about it. What Ham did can be seen when
it is noted what his brothers did. They refused to look on
their father in his nakedness. They covered him, showing
compassion for their father as well as respect and charity.
James writes, "Let him know, that he which converteth the
sinner from the error of his way, shall save a soul from death,
and shall hide a multitude of sins." This does not mean that
when I lead a soul to Christ my own sins will be hidden.
But when I win another to the Lord, I am to cover his past
and his sins and never talk about them.

Some may wonder whether the curse pronounced upon
Ham has any bearing on some particular race of people.
No! The curse upon Canaan had no biological or racial
significance. It has a spiritual connotation and indicates a
solemn warning to all who indulge in gossip. The curse of

Ham will fall upon those who publish what is hurtful or embarrassing to someone else. If I know things which are detrimental to someone, I am to cover them up. I am not to speak of such! When I take advantage of any man when he is helpless, even if he has brought that state upon himself, I am in grave danger of bringing the curse of Ham upon myself. Gossiping is a form of cruelty in which a Christian should have no part.

Chapter Twelve

THE JUDGMENT OF GOD

(Genesis 9-11)

The Bible shows that we are utterly dependent upon God. The air we breathe, the water we drink, the food we eat, even the heartbeat that keeps the blood circulating in our bodies are beyond our control. God made this world: He made man. He keeps and maintains everything. God created all things and is sovereign over the whole world. He planned the laws men must follow. In some limited ways men make up their own rules for guidance, but there are things in nature, in the universe, and in humanity that no one can change.

Living in this world is a good deal like living in a countryside where each road and each path leads somewhere. One highway leads north to Winnipeg, Canada; another leads to Chicago, Illinois. So one road leads to New York, while still another goes to California. All such highways have destinations. They lead somewhere. This country road leads to the farm where the Smiths live, but another road leads to the Browns' farm. Even paths in the yard lead to a garden or to the barn or to the house. Even so, a man's conduct leads to certain consequences. The law of harvest never changes. Just so, in the wisdom of God the laws of nature do not change. The first mile of the highway to Chicago remains the highway to Chicago after ten or twenty, a hundred or three hundred miles. Chicago was the destination of this highway from its very beginning. Conduct is like that.

Action may take time to arrive at its consequence, but God knows from the beginning when I act in a certain way where my conduct will lead. God does not have to figure this out; He knows my every thought. He knows all things. In my living I may think of many things I never get to do, but God knows them all. A wrong thought can lead to a wrong act. John writes, "He that hateth his brother is a murderer." Hating is not specifically murder, as we know, but hating can lead to murder. God knows where our thoughts can lead us. He knows the significance of our thoughts.

It is emphasized in the Bible that God will destroy evil. Does this mean He is arbitrary? When we plant a rosebush, we know that it will need proper soil and water and sunshine in order to grow. If we give it no moisture, it will die. Did God kill it? No, not in that sense. Or let us consider a growing tree. If its roots are attacked by some rodent, the tree will die. That's a law of nature. Does this make God arbitrary? We never saw a flower that did not wither or a blade of grass that did not dry out. Death is universal in nature. It is a law of nature that if I take poison into my body I will kill my body, even if I had no intention to do so.

So far as my soul is concerned it too needs certain conditions under which to prosper. One of these is the favor of God. This I receive through obedience to Him. When my soul is obedient to God, I will be like a tree planted by rivers of water. If my soul is not obedient to God, if I live contrary to His will, it will be with me like cutting off a tree. "The soul that sinneth. it shall die." Now the consequences of sin are just as real for the soul as the breaking of natural laws are for the body. Suppose a man climbs a mountain in stormy weather and falls three hundred feet to his death. Does this mean that God killed him? No! The man need not have climbed under these conditions. God does not violate the processes of nature or the laws of the universe that He has established. Consequences in the spiritual realm are equally real.

It was in the plan of God that Adam and Eve should obey Him in order to live in the Garden of Eden. The way a fish needs water in which to swim, the way a bird needs air to fly, or a man needs air to breathe, so man needs to obey God to live in harmony with his Creator. When Adam sinned, death became inevitable. In the case of Cain and Abel we saw that worship of God must come from a willing heart. Why? Because God created man in this way. When we come into the presence of God, He looks into our hearts. If our hearts are not right in His eyes, God will not accept our presence nor what we bring. No gift will clear us. When God looked at Abel, He accepted his offering. When He looked into the heart of Cain, his offering was not acceptable. God said to Cain, "If thou doest well, shalt thou not be accepted?" Envy is wrong, jealousy is wrong, and murder is wrong. The judgment upon Cain was not imposed on him arbitrarily. The judgment of the Flood was an inevitable result of the wickedness and evil which was rampant in the world. It only proves again that the "law of the harvest" can never be broken.

In the same way, trust in God inevitably brings with it blessing and salvation. This is the spiritual law of harvest. Trust and obedience bring life and blessing, just as surely as disobedience brings death.

Another important revelation of truth is found in the building of the Tower of Babel.

> And the whole earth was of one language, and of one speech. And it came to pass, as they journeyed from the east, that they found a plain in the land of Shinar; and they dwelt there. And they said one to another, Go to, let us make brick, and burn them throughly. And they had brick for stone, and slime had they for mortar. And they said, Go to, let us build us a city and a tower, whose top may reach unto heaven; and let us make us a name, lest we be scattered abroad upon the face of the whole earth (Gen. 11:1-4).

One thing to be noticed in this story is that the building of this tower was the original classic community enterprise on record. All the people were engaged in this building project. This was certainly a wonderful example of co-operation and unity. Even today, if people in this world got together and agreed with one another, they could accomplish a whole lot more than they can when they are separated. There is no doubt about that. These people who proceeded to build a city and a tower were inspired by potential mutual benefit. They wanted to make a name for themselves by a monument which would be notable. They wanted to dwell in this city and avoid being scattered throughout the whole world. All were challenged by this ambitious plan. "Let us build us a city and a tower, whose top may reach unto heaven." These people were guided by practical efficiency. They planned for the bricks and the mortar they would use. In other words they made all the necessary preliminary arrangements to achieve their purpose.

Then we read, "The Lord came down to see the city and the tower" (11:5). God knew their thoughts from afar. He knew that if they succeeded in this ambitious enterprise, their pride and arrogance would know no bounds. They would feel no desire to worship Him their Maker, but rather the creature. Their pride would separate them from the only true source of all blessing. Then it is written, "Let us . . . confound their language, that they may not understand one another's speech" (11:7). This act of God caused men to disagree "and they left off to build the city," and were scattered throughout the world.

It is important and vital that men understand the same language if they would work together. Yet it is so universal to have difference in speech. Even in one country many dialects may be spoken. There are at least seventeen different dialects spoken in China. When I was in Taiwan, I was told that ten aboriginal tribes lived in the mountains, and each tribe spoke a different dialect. They cannot understand each other. When it comes to world affairs it would be a boon to all who work for unity among nations if there were no language barrier. Here in this country we have the common problem of getting along with the various organizations, because even though they speak the same common language they do not agree in their thinking. Actually disagreement can take place even in the home, because this is human nature. This is true all over the world. We may note in passing the striking fact that at Pentecost (Acts 2:6-11) all nationalities were able to hear the Gospel in "their own tongue." What a blessing to be had in Christ!

There is a real contrast between these people who wanted to vaunt their own superiority by building a city and the man Abraham, who was called to obey God in the next chapter. It is written of him in the Book of Hebrews that "he looked for a city which hath foundations whose builder and maker is God." Whereas the men of Babel planned to build a city, this man looked for one whose builder was God. This is very significant, for it points to a man whom God called out from all that he had in himself, and who obeyed God. This was the man to whom God promised that in him all the nations of the world would be blessed. It is noteworthy that when men tried by their own efforts to insure their unity the result was that they were scattered abroad; but when this individual man was called to leave all he had in himself that he might receive what God would give him, he received the promise that "in thee and in thy seed shall all nations be blessed."

The men of Babel set out to *achieve* in their own strength and failed; Abraham yielded everything that he might *receive* what God had prepared to give to him, and he was blessed.

Chapter Thirteen

THE COVENANT WITH ABRAHAM

(Genesis 12-13)

God's Word deals with the nature of man and of men's dealings in human affairs. Men take pride in their possessions, in the things they have worked for and saved for. But, now, when are possessions of value? Is it not when these are necessary and vital? What does man actually need? First, all men need life. Man can neither earn it nor keep it one moment longer than God decrees. Obviously man is constantly dependent on God's providence, which supplies every physical and spiritual need. Everything man has that is good comes from the hand of God as a gift. Even what is needed for daily living are things that are available. Even my place of work, my tools, my office equipment and machinery, everything I handle is there for my use, even though I am personally not responsible for all this. I could not even get along without the fire and the police departments, and the Public Health service, to look after my interests. On every hand I, like all others, take for granted all the services which are at my command even though I did not provide for them.

In Genesis we will see that this is also true spiritually. In the building of the Tower of Babel was to be seen the limitation of human effort. Those people had great plans. They tried to build something lasting, but it came to nothing. In contrast, Abraham, who followed the guidance of God, was the pioneer of faith.

Now the Lord had said unto Abram, Get thee out of

thy country, and from thy kindred, and from thy father's
house, unto a land that I will shew thee: And I will make
of thee a great nation, and I will bless thee, and make thy
name great; and thou shalt be a blessing: And I will bless
them that bless thee, and curse him that curseth thee:
and in thee shall all families of the earth be blessed
(Gen. 12:1-3).

Here is God's call and promise to Abraham recorded for
our learning. In himself Abraham was not different; he
wanted just exactly what the men of Babel wanted. The
difference was in their attitude: where they were motivated
by pride, Abraham was motivated by faith. The men of
Babel wanted security. They wanted to be safe and sure
and they wanted to make for themselves a great name. They
worked to get this security and satisfaction, and they failed.
That was the vain effort of man in his own power. Abraham
believed and obeyed God, that he might receive security and
satisfaction. Actually this is the whole story of the Bible:
when men believe the promises of God they will receive
them.

"Get thee out of thy country, and from thy kindred, and
from thy father's house" means "Break off everything,
leave everything behind you, and come where I will lead
you." Abraham had first of all to learn that he must not
cling to anything, not even his own strength and ability.
He was instructed to put away self, and go "unto a land that
I will shew thee." God had something better in store for
him than he could ever earn for himself. This is the primary
phase of receiving the blessing of God as revealed in the
Bible. As we empty our hands in denying self, God will
take charge. "I will make of thee a great nation, and I will
bless thee, and make thy name great; and thou shalt be a
blessing." This was exactly what the men of Babel had
planned and worked for. They had said, "Let us make us a
name." In Hebrews 11:8-16 it is revealed that the blessing
of God comes not only upon Abraham, but upon anyone
who wants to receive it as he did. This is the very essence
of the Gospel.

All who follow in the footsteps of Abraham declare that

they too seek a country and "a city which hath foundations, whose builder and maker is God." They confess that they are "pilgrims and strangers" on this earth. God promises His personal care to all that trust Him. To say that Abraham believed God is much more than saying that he believed that God is. Abraham believed that he could take God at His word, and he believed His promises. He believed without doubt that what God promised, He was also able to perform. He went out from his home, from his father's house, and from his kindred, not knowing whither he went. Abraham did not know what any morrow would bring forth, but he went confidently, for he trusted God.

> But without faith it is impossible to please him: for he that cometh to God must believe that he is, and that he is a rewarder of them that diligently seek him (Heb. 11:6).

It is not enough to believe in the existence of God if we want His blessing. To all who do not believe in the existence of God, I would say, "Go out and look at the stars, look at the mountains, look at the rolling waves of the ocean, and at the wide plains. Look at the land, the lakes, the rivers, the birds, and the beasts of the field. Look at human beings, and their potential for good and evil." I remember years ago when our children were small, I happened to be sitting at an open window. Outside the window two of our children were talking. The little girl, who was three, asked her brother, who was five, "What makes the leaves on the trees move?" The boy with his superior knowledge said, "The wind." The little girl persisted, "What makes the wind move?" Her brother said without a moment's hesitation, "God." By the way, that little boy has grown up to be an electronics engineer. He has been on the faculty as a professor of electro-magnetics. He is studying space engineering problems, but I am confident that if he were asked today the same question, he would give the same answer, "God." He would know much more of natural processes, but back of all the hidden factors involved, there is "God." The Bible has a word for those who doubt the reality of

God: "The fool hath said in his heart there is no God." But believing that God exists does not bring peace to the heart and assurance to the soul. James writes, "The devils also believe, and tremble."

No doubt many people want the blessing of God who do not know how to find it. The first step to blessing is to seek the mind of God. It is as I read God's Word and pray and meditate on it that His Holy Spirit will guide and direct me into His will. Abraham not only believed the promises of God, but he obeyed God even though he did not know what each day might bring forth. It is here again that many people falter. They are actually grieved in their hearts because the blessing of God is not evident in their lives. The fact of the matter is that they are not willing to change, to be different. Abraham held back nothing. God was more important to him than his father and his kindred. Think of it! This was the nature of his faith even under most severe testing. We could all understand how a man might be called to leave evil company. When a man has done wrong, or when he is involved in a sinful situation, it is easy to see why he should be willing to change. But with Abraham this was not the case. He was called from his home and his belongings to enter into the will and the blessing of God.

Abraham's dealings with his nephew, Lot, further reveal that he was ready to give up any advantage for the sake of peace. Lot, like Abraham, had great flocks of sheep and herds of cattle. It happened that the herdsmen of Abraham and the herdsmen of Lot quarreled over the best pasture for the animals. There was not enough good pasture for all, and the servants argued with each other. Abraham felt that separation was the only solution, and his procedure has become a classic. It is an example to all believers.

> And Abram said unto Lot, Let there be no strife, I pray thee, between me and thee, and between my herdmen and thy herdmen; for we be brethren. Is not the whole land before thee? separate thyself, I pray thee, from me: if thou wilt take the left hand, then I will go to the right;

or if thou depart to the right hand, then I will go to the left (Gen. 13:8-9).

When Lot was given this opportunity he chose the well watered valley of Jordan; Abraham took what was left, which was a plateau in the mountains.

The first thing Abraham did was to build an altar to worship God. Nowhere do we find a record of Lot building an altar. Abraham separated from Lot so that there would be no more quarreling among their herdsmen. But this did not mean that Abraham lost interest in Lot. The records show that Abraham later interceded in Lot's behalf. What a challenge to believers to intercede for their children and for others who are outside the blessing of God!

Chapter Fourteen

THE FAITH OF ABRAHAM

(Genesis 14-23)

No one expects unbelievers to live unselfish lives. This does not excuse them, but their selfishness can be understood. However, it is hard to accept when a person who professes to be a Christian is selfish. In Genesis there is an actual example of this in Lot. He can be thought of as a "twilight" believer because twilight is a time of day when it is neither day nor night. Unfortunately there are some Christians like that. One cannot say that they are not Christians, but neither can one say that they are what they profess to be.

Abraham's nephew, Lot, came with him when they set forth from Ur of the Chaldees as God led them. Abraham's father was an idol maker. Yet with idol worship all around him Abraham believed in the Invisible God, Creator of the heavens and the earth, and Giver of all things. Lot also was a grown man of means; he had flocks and herds of his own. Here were two men in the pagan world whose common bond was not only that they were kinsmen but that they both had faith in God. The reason for Abraham's greatness was his obedience to God. Lot's life actually resulted in loss and shame and this was due to his basic selfishness.

Results in living are never haphazard. They do not occur by chance. There is always a reason for them. When Lot chose the fertile valley for his grazing, we see the first indication of weakness in his character. In making this choice, Lot ignored the spiritual peril which would beset him when he chose to live near the city of exceedingly wicked men. Thus Lot's trouble began because he was covetous. When anyone wants the best and the most for himself, he is moving into trouble. The Scripture says, "Seekest thou great things for thyself? Seek them not." Lot's desire for personal advantage and gain blinded his judgment. The next indication of his weakness can be seen as he became careless in his associations. He knew of the wickedness of the men of Sodom, and yet he "dwelled in the cities of the plain."

Sodom was a large city where cattle could be sold and money was to be made. Because of the wealth of Sodom it was often besieged and raided.

During one of these raids Lot was captured with the Sodomites by the enemies of that city, for by now he too "dwelt in Sodom." He had chosen the worldly road to success, and now he had lost his possessions and was in danger of losing his life. A refugee came to Abraham and told him that Lot had been captured and carried away with the people of Sodom. Abraham immediately organized a rescue party and pursued the enemy. With his 318 servants he managed to liberate Lot and the people of Sodom with all their goods. The king of Sodom wanted to pay Abraham for this deliverance, but Abraham would not take his money. Then he offered Abraham the loot they had won in battle, but he would not touch a thing lest anyone say that the king of Sodom had made him rich. He would not accept any personal profit from this particular experience.

Although he was separated from Lot, Abraham did not abandon his nephew to the consequences of his own actions. In the time of his extremity Lot received help from the spiritual man Abraham. After he was rescued Lot remained in Sodom despite his experience. Apparently living there was profitable for him, so he stayed on. He became an honored man in the community. "He sat in the gate of Sodom," which means that he was on the town council and was one of the leading citizens in the community. Peter writes, "Lot vexed his righteous soul daily with the ungodly deeds that these people committed." Thus we see that Lot was grieved with their ungodliness, but he did not leave them.

The wickedness of Sodom continued to increase until God decided to destroy the city. God revealed to Abraham the judgment which He would execute upon Sodom. Abraham prayed that God would spare the city, if there were fifty righteous people in it (Gen. 18:20-33). He prayed again and again until finally he asked whether God would not spare the city if there were ten righteous in it. But the wickedness of that city was so great that not even ten righteous people were to be found there. However, God did rescue Lot and his wife and his two daughters from the destruction which followed. He sent two angels to lead them to safety before the utter annihilation of this evil city.

This account is impressive because of Abraham's repeated intercessory prayer. It is deeply moving to see the grace of God, which did not forsake him in a time of great calamity. Another lesson is found in Lot's attempt to persuade his sons-in-law to leave the city, after being warned of its coming destruction. We read: "He seemed as one that mocked unto his sons in law." What a sad, sad situation when a person's own testimony to his family carries no weight! The husbands of Lot's two daughters just laughed at him. As a result these two men perished in the flames that engulfed the city. On their way out of the city, Lot's wife looked back at the city and was turned into a pillar of salt. So in the end Lot lost all the things he had gone to Sodom to acquire. This is the fate of any "twilight" Christian who lives without power or joy, and without a testimony to those who are dying all around him. How different from Abraham this was!

"Abraham believed God, and it was counted to him for righteousness." This is the well-known testimony of Scripture for all believers. Throughout the Bible it is written again and again that Abraham was a man of faith. Paul presents Abraham as the pioneer believer, calling him "the father of us all."

> Therefore it is of faith, that it might be by grace; to the end the promise might be sure to all the seed; not to that

only which is of the law, but to that also which is of the faith of Abraham; who is the father of us all, (As it is written, I have made thee a father of many nations,) before him whom he believed, even God, who quickeneth the dead, and calleth those things which be not as though they were. Who against hope believed in hope, that he might become the father of many nations, according to that which was spoken, So shall thy seed be. And being not weak in faith, he considered not his own body now dead, when he was about an hundred years old, neither yet the deadness of Sarah's womb: He staggered not at the promise of God through unbelief; but was strong in faith, giving glory to God; And being fully persuaded that, what he had promised, he was able also to perform. And therefore it was imputed to him for righteousness. Now it was not written for his sake alone, that it was imputed to him; But for us also, to whom it shall be imputed, if we believe on him that raised up Jesus our Lord from the dead; Who was delivered for our offences, and was raised again for our justification (Rom. 4:16-25).

In this passage is found the classic definition and description of Abraham's faith, "Being fully persuaded that, what he had promised, he was able also to perform."

It can be helpful to remember that in Abraham's day there were no churches nor Scriptures to encourage him. But he had an inner guidance in his own soul. He had an awareness of the presence of God. In that day God spoke directly: He revealed Himself directly to Abraham, whose faith was centered in God. Abraham's faith was not grounded in human nature nor in natural processes. He did not depend on faith in his own ability and intelligence. Abraham knew God and because he trusted Him he left his home and his relatives and went where God would lead him.

In the New Testament is the record of these words of our Lord Jesus Christ, "If any man will be my disciple, let him deny himself, take up his cross and follow me." On another occasion He said:

And every one that hath forsaken houses, or brethren, or sisters, or father, or mother, or wife, or children, or lands, for my name's sake, shall receive an hundredfold, and shall inherit everlasting life (Matt. 19:29).

In other words, when God calls, nothing must stand in the way. Nothing else has priority when spiritual values are at stake. Some people feel that if they have confidence in themselves they will be successful in whatever they undertake. The Bible teaches that our confidence must rest in God. Our faith must be centered in Him. In obedience to the will of God, Abraham separated himself first from his kindred and later from his nephew Lot. Obstensibly this was done to avoid tension. Abraham did not want conflict between their servants. This is the way it appears on the surface, but we can be sure that the hand of the Lord was in this separation. When Abraham gave Lot the choice of the best grazing lands, he was trusting God to watch over his affairs. Because of his complete faith in God, he was blessed beyond human understanding.

Chapter Fifteen

ISHMAEL

(Genesis 16-21)

God promised Abraham that his seed would be as innumerable as the stars in the heavens and the sand on the seashore. But Abraham had no son. God also had promised that Abraham's wife Sarah would bear him a son. As the years went by without the fulfillment of this promise, Sarah took things into her own hands. Feeling that her time for childbearing was passed, she persuaded Abraham to marry her Egyptian maid, Hagar (Gen. 16:3). When Hagar discovered that she was to have a child, she began to look down upon her mistress and "despised" her. When Sarah told this to Abraham, he said to her, "Behold, thy maid is in thy hand; do to her as it pleaseth thee. And when Sarai dealt hardly with her, she fled from her face." Evidently Sarah asserted herself as mistress and undertook to put Hagar in her place as her maid, and so we read that Hagar fled into the wilderness until she came to a fountain of water.

> And the angel of the Lord found her by a fountain of water in the wilderness, by the fountain in the way to Shur. And he said, Hagar, Sarai's maid, whence camest thou? and whither wilt thou go? And she said, I flee from the face of my mistress Sarai. And the angel of the Lord said unto her, Return to thy mistress, and submit thyself under her hands (Gen. 16:7-9).

There is important truth revealed in Hagar's experience. Some people are called on to endure hard things. Hagar not only had to face harsh treatment from her mistress, but the angel of the Lord told her that her son "will be a wild man; his hand will be against every man, and every man's hand against him." Despite his quarrelsome temperament, this man was to become the father of a vast multitude of people. When Hagar's son was born, she called him "Ishmael," even as the angel of the Lord had instructed her to do.

When Abraham was one hundred years old his faith in God's promise was rewarded, and Sarah bore him a son, and they called him Isaac, which literally translated means, "God hath prepared laughter for me." Sarah's incredulous laughter at the time when God told her that she would have a son after she had passed the age of childbearing was now turned into laughter of pure joy. As time passed, her joy was marred by the scoffing of Ishmael. "And Sarah saw the son of Hagar the Egyptian, which she had born unto Abraham, mocking." Again Sarah came to Abraham and told him what had to be done.

> Wherefore she said unto Abraham, Cast out this bond-woman and her son: for the son of this bondwoman shall not be heir with my son, even with Isaac. And the thing was very grievous in Abraham's sight because of his son (21:10-11).

Abraham loved Ishmael and to cast him and his mother out of his house was something he was not ready to do.

> And God said unto Abraham, Let it not be grievous in thy sight because of the lad, and because of thy bond-woman; in all that Sarah hath said unto thee, hearken unto her voice; for in Isaac shall thy seed be called. And also of the son of the bondwoman will I make a nation, because he is thy seed (21:12-13).

This must have been a very painful time. Abraham loved Ishmael, who was his own son. Incidentally, Ishmael was at least thirteen years of age at this time and living as became the son of a man of wealth and renown. What a tragic experience for him and his mother to be suddenly deprived of everything they had come to accept as their due!

Hagar and the boy departed early in the morning and wandered in the wilderness of Beersheba. Abraham had given them food and water for their journey, but as they went on they ran out of water. Now they faced death by thirst. Hagar was more able to endure the heat than Ishmael, so she placed him in the shade of a shrub and walked "a good way off, as it were a bowshot: for she said, Let me not see the death of the child. And she sat over against him, and lift up her voice, and wept." How utterly bleak and hard her lot appeared! Hagar was too spent with sorrow to pray, but Ishmael cried out to the God of his father Abraham, "And the angel of God called to Hagar out of heaven, and said unto her, What aileth thee, Hagar? fear not; for God hath heard the voice of the lad where he is." I wonder if we can fully appreciate the fact that Ishmael, this quarrelsome boy, knew about God. Ishmael had been brought up by Abraham. He knew that God answers prayer. It was right to turn to Him in his extremity. When Hagar heard the voice of the angel say unto her, "Fear not, for God hath heard the voice of the lad," her sorrow vanished, her courage revived. "And God opened her eyes, and she saw a well of water; and she went, and filled the bottle with water, and gave the lad drink. And God was with the lad; and he grew, and dwelt in the wilderness, and became an archer. And he dwelt in the wilderness of Paran." According to God's promise, Ishmael became very rich and prosperous.

Surely our faith is strengthened as we study and learn more about God and His dealings with men. Surely His mercy is inexhaustible in His guidance and in His offer of salvation, which is to all men. God will not save arbitrarily. He will not take man and push him into heaven. God calls all men, but men must respond to His call. God offers salvation, but unless we accept, it will pass us by. Parents have a powerful influence on the lives of their children. So it was with Ishmael. He prayed because his father Abraham prayed. He expected help from God because he had seen Abraham's prayers answered.

It will be the common rule that non-churchgoing parents will have children who do not go to church. When parents do not pray, it follows almost invariably that their children do not pray. Praying is something readily learned from parents. How well this was demonstrated in the life of Abraham!

God made a covenant with Abraham and sealed it with a ceremony, namely the rite of circumcision. This was to be a constant reminder of the promise of God, that He would extend His blessing from the father to the son.

> And I will establish my covenant between me and thee and thy seed after thee in their generations for an everlasting covenant, to be a God unto thee, and to thy seed after thee. And I will give unto thee, and to thy seed after thee, the land wherein thou art a stranger, all the land of Canaan, for an everlasting possession; and I will be their God (17:7-8).

Many Christian churches practice a ceremony called "infant baptism," with the thought in mind that in this rite the infant becomes a partaker of the blessing of the Lord. They have in mind that when believing parents present their children to God, He will bless the faith of the parents. The rite of baptism does not guarantee that the child will grow up to be a believer, but it does show the intention of the parents to bring up their children in the nurture and admonition of the Lord.

Chapter Sixteen

ISAAC

(Genesis 21-28)

God created the world in such a way that the natural processes will always be the same. When a man plants beans, he will harvest beans. When he plants potatoes, he will harvest potatoes, regardless of whether he is an honest man or a crook, a believer or an unbeliever. The laws of nature operate without regard to the quality of the persons involved. Spiritual processes operate entirely within the relationship which exists between the believer and God. It is written, "According to your faith, be it unto you."

God promised Abraham that his descendants would be as innumerable as the stars in heaven and the sand on the seashore. God's promise was sure, but the time of fulfillment was uncertain. For Abraham and Sarah the years of waiting seemed endless. God's people often have to wait and often become impatient. Abraham and Sarah's impatience in waiting for the promised heir is evidenced by the fact that Sarah gave her maid Hagar to be Abraham's wife that she might bear him a son.

After the birth of Ishmael, Hagar's son, God appeared again to Abraham.

> And God said, Sarah thy wife shall bear thee a son indeed; and thou shalt call his name Isaac: and I will establish my covenant with him for an everlasting covenant, and with his seed after him (Gen. 17:19).

Nothing is impossible with God! God will always carry

95

out His promises. In the realm of the spirit His promises operate according to grace. The fulfillment of these promises is wholly dependent on His power and mercy. In the realm of nature the integrity and the law of God prevail. There is a real difference between these two realms, and this emphasizes the great truth that flesh and blood cannot inherit the kingdom of God. In other words, man in his natural state could never obey the will of God: he needs all the spiritual riches in Christ Jesus made available to him by the grace of God.

All this was demonstrated in the birth of Isaac. God's promise to Abraham required the operation of the grace of God beyond the natural. In referring to Abraham, Paul wrote:

> Who against hope believed in hope, that he might become the father of many nations, according to that which was spoken, So shall thy seed be. And being not weak in faith, he considered not his own body now dead, when he was about an hundred years old, neither yet the deadness of Sarah's womb: He staggered not at the promise of God through unbelief; but was strong in faith, giving glory to God; And being fully persuaded that, what he had promised, he was able also to perform (Rom. 4:18-21).

God honors faith. He brings His will to pass over nature, beyond nature and above nature in supernatural power. This power must be recognized if the Bible is to be understood. God can and will do far beyond "all that we ask or think."

Many people are able to believe that God can bless and save, yet often these same people refuse to believe that God will send destruction. The Bible is very clear in teaching that because of wickedness God will destroy. There are several classic examples of this in the Bible. First of all, there was the flood which completely destroyed all men because their sin was so great that the thoughts of men's hearts were only evil continually. It was so with Sodom and Gomorrah, when those two cities were utterly destroyed. Pharaoh, who pursued the Israelites, perished in the Red Sea with all his host. There is also the case of Korah and all his company, who rebelled against God and His chosen servant Moses: "the earth opened her mouth and swallowed them up." There is also the account of Achan, who stole of the spoils of battle in the siege of Jericho. These were not to be touched, but he buried them under his tent. He was put to death by stoning for his sin. Nadab and Abihu were the sons of Aaron the High Priest, who were consumed with fire which came out of the altar because they had taken strange fire, contrary to the Word of God, into the tabernacle. Many more instances of utter and complete destruction meted out by God are recorded in the Old Testament.

Some will say that in the New Testament there are no similar cases recorded, but this is not true. These words were spoken by our Lord Jesus Christ in stern warning of possible judgment.

> But whoso shall offend one of these little ones which believe in me, it were better for him that a millstone were hanged about his neck, and that he were drowned in the depth of the sea. Woe unto the world because of offences! for it must needs be that offences come; but woe to that man by whom the offence cometh! Wherefore if thy hand or thy foot offend thee, cut them off, and cast them from thee: it is better for thee to enter into life halt or maimed, rather than having two hands or two feet to be cast into everlasting fire (Matt. 18:6-8).

These hard words leave no doubt about the destruction of the wicked. Peter wrote, "But the heavens and the earth, which are now, by the same word are kept in store, reserved unto fire against the day of judgment and perdition of ungodly men" (2 Pet. 3:7). The words of Paul are written in the same vein:

> And to you who are troubled rest with us, when the Lord Jesus shall be revealed from heaven with his mighty angels, In flaming fire taking vengeance on them that know not God, and that obey not the gospel of our Lord Jesus Christ: Who shall be punished with everlasting destruction from the presence of the Lord, and from the glory of his power (2 Thess. 1:7-9).

It is always saddening to think about the unbelievers

who will not be warned by such passages of Scripture, which clearly show that God will destroy all who willfully reject his offer of salvation and eternal life. It is comforting to remember that God is willing to be gracious. In the destruction of Sodom, Lot was saved for Abraham's sake. "God remembered Abraham, and sent Lot out of the midst of the overthrow, when he overthrew the cities" (Gen. 19:29).

While it is true that God has no pleasure in the death of the wicked, there is not the least doubt in the world that the plan of God provides a place of eternal punishment, into which Satan and all his angels and all who have rejected the Gospel will be thrown. No rational argument can ever upset or contradict this plain teaching of Scripture.

In fact, no rational argument can ever alter the truth as it is written in the Scripture. Besides the natural world which God created, there is the spiritual world into which believers are born. The spiritual world is in itself eternal and is as real as the natural world in which we live. It is helpful to remember that a Christian is involved in both "the natural" and "the spiritual" world. Paul writes, "Howbeit that was not first which is spiritual, but that which is natural; and afterward that which is spiritual" (1 Cor. 15:46). Every human being is born first into the natural world. When anyone believes and accepts Christ's substitutionary atonement on Calvary, he is born again into the spiritual world. Then follows for the Christian the rather strenuous exercise of belonging to the spiritual while living in this natural world, where he is to be a shining light in the midst of people who walk in darkness.

In discussing this situation for the Christian, Paul writes:

> For it is written, that Abraham had two sons, the one by a bondmaid, the other by a freewoman. But he who was of the bondwoman was born after the flesh; but he of the freewoman was by promise (Gal. 4:22-23).

There is much to learn here. Isaac's whole experience grows out of the fact that he is the child that God gave to Abraham and Sarah by promise. According to the flesh, this

child would not have been born. He was the child of
promise. In a similar way in the New Testament is written
the record of John the Baptist, who also was born in the fulfillment of God's promise to Zacharias.

Isaac is an example, a type of the born-again Christian.
He walked in the footsteps of his father Abraham, the man
of faith. It could be said that he was born by spiritual
power. What happened to Abraham, whom God so signally
honored, can be understood because of spiritual realities
such as heaven. It is so easy to think of earth, for it is all
around us. Heaven is invisible, but it is just as real as the
visible earth. The invisible belongs to God as much as the
earth because He created them both.

The word *earth* refers to this world, which is commonly
called "nature," where all processes operate according to
law. "Whatsoever a man soweth, that shall he also reap."
While both the sowing and the reaping go on in this world,
there is another world in the realm of the spiritual. In the
natural world men reap what they sow. In the spiritual
world men receive what God gives quite aside from anything men do. In the flesh, which is human nature, men are
motivated into actions which will bring desired consequences, and in which they often take great pride. In the
spiritual realm, events occur according to the grace of God,
to whom all praise belongs. When Abraham first received
God's promise of a son, he expected Sarah would bear one
soon. This was a natural expectation. But God withheld
this son until he was born in a supernatural way. In a very
real sense Isaac was the gift of God to Abraham.

Through Isaac God proceeded to the supreme test of
Abraham's faith.

> And it came to pass after these things, that God did
> tempt Abraham, and said unto him, Abraham: and he
> said, Behold, here I am. And he said, Take now thy son,
> thine only son Isaac, whom thou lovest, and get thee into
> the land of Moriah; and offer him there for a burnt offer-
> ing upon one of the mountains which I will tell thee of.
> And Abraham rose up early in the morning, and saddled
> his ass, and took two of his young men with him, and
> Isaac his son, and clave the wood for the burnt offering,

and rose up, and went unto the place of which God had
told him (Gen. 22:1-3).

The Epistle to the Hebrews gives an insight into the un-
shakeable faith of Abraham:

> By faith Abraham, when he was tried, offered up Isaac:
> and he that had received the promises offered up his only
> begotten son, of whom it was said, That in Isaac shall
> thy seed be called: Accounting that God was able to
> raise him up, even from the dead; from whence also he
> received him in a figure (Heb. 11:17-19).

Abraham did not falter at this request which seemed so
contrary to God's promise. He was not hindered by doubts
nor any apprehension of what lay ahead for him. God had
spoken and he obeyed. He still believed that in Isaac he
would be blessed.

Although the promise of God is always sure, the procedure God will follow is often obscure. Belief in God is not
based upon the believer's understanding. The Christian
should seek to know His promises, and then trust Him implicitly for their fulfillment. Abraham did not hesitate. He
obeyed God.

> And they came to the place which God had told him of;
> and Abraham built an altar there, and laid the wood in
> order, and bound Isaac his son, and laid him on the altar
> upon the wood. And Abraham stretched forth his hand,
> and took the knife to slay his son. And the angel of the
> Lord called unto him out of heaven, and said, Abraham,
> Abraham: and he said, Here am I. And he said, Lay not
> thine hand upon the lad, neither do thou any thing unto
> him: for now I know that thou fearest God, seeing thou
> hast not withheld thy son, thine only son from me (Gen.
> 22:9-12).

It is when a believer is ready to give up self that he will
receive the peace of God. When I am willing to lay all upon
the altar, the blessing of God will be my daily portion.

Chapter Seventeen

THE WISDOM OF ISAAC

(Genesis 26)

In Genesis 24 there is written the record of a very important and meaningful event in the life of Abraham and his son Isaac. Abraham had been blessed with great material riches and was now concerned that his son Isaac should marry a bride of whom he could approve. With careful instruction he sent his chief servant on a mission into his old homeland to find a bride for Isaac.

> And I will make thee swear by the Lord, the God of heaven, and the God of the earth, that thou shalt not take a wife unto my son of the daughters of the Canaanites, among whom I dwell: But thou shalt go unto my country, and to my kindred, and take a wife unto my son Isaac (Gen. 24:3-4).

Abraham did not want Isaac to return to the land from which he himself had come, because God had promised to bless him in the country in which he dwelt.

> The Lord God of heaven, which took me from my father's house, and from the land of my kindred, and which spake unto me, and that sware unto me, saying, Unto thy seed will I give this land; he shall send his angel before thee, and thou shalt take a wife unto my son from thence. And if the woman will not be willing to follow thee, then thou shalt be clear from this my oath: only bring not my son thither again (24:7-8).

In this incident in the Old Testament there is a profound application for Christians.

Spiritually speaking every human being is born into this world in the flesh, but when anyone accepts Christ he enters into the realm of the spirit, and does not remain in his human nature in which the flesh controls the spirit. The Church, that is all believers, is spoken of in the Bible as "the bride of Christ." In the Genesis account the bride was to leave her country and come away from her kindred to become the bride of Isaac. Here is a type of the call of the Gospel. In response to the Gospel a man must leave the situation he is in, in order to come to the Lord. More specifically he must leave his old nature, he must leave himself, in answering the call of the Gospel.

The story unfolds to record that the servant of Abraham prayed for divine guidance.

> And he said, O Lord God of my master Abraham, I pray thee, send me good speed this day, and shew kindness unto my master Abraham. Behold, I stand here by the well of water; and the daughters of the men of the city come out to draw water: And let it come to pass, that the damsel to whom I shall say, Let down thy pitcher, I pray thee, that I may drink; and she shall say, Drink, and I will give thy camels drink also: let the same be she that thou hast appointed for thy servant Isaac; and thereby shall I know that thou hast shewed kindness unto my master (24:12-14).

It is refreshing to read how wonderfully and explicitly God answered his prayer.

> And it came to pass, before he had done speaking, that, behold, Rebekah came out, who was born to Bethuel, son of Milcah, the wife of Nahor, Abraham's brother, with her pitcher upon her shoulder. And the damsel was very fair to look upon, a virgin, neither had any man known her: and she went down to the well, and filled her pitcher, and came up. And the servant ran to meet her, and said, Let me, I pray thee, drink a little water of thy pitcher. And she said, Drink, my lord: and she hasted, and let down her pitcher upon her hand, and gave him drink. And when she had done giving him drink, she said, I will draw water for thy camels also, until they have done drinking. And she hasted, and emptied her pitcher into the trough, and ran again unto the well to draw water, and drew for all his camels (24:15-20).

pened. He was taken aback and bewildered at the instant answer to his prayer.

> And it came to pass, as the camels had done drinking, that the man took a golden earring of half a shekel weight, and two bracelets for her hands of ten shekels weight of gold; And said, Whose daughter art thou? tell me, I pray thee: is there room in thy father's house for us to lodge in? And she said unto him, I am the daughter of Bethuel the son of Milcah, which she bare unto Nahor. She said moreover unto him, We have both straw and provender enough, and room to lodge in. And the man bowed down his head, and worshipped the Lord. And he said, Blessed be the Lord God of my master Abraham, who hath not left destitute my master of his mercy and his truth: I being in the way, the Lord led me to the house of my master's brethren. And the damsel ran, and told them of her mother's house these things (24:22-28).

As we read the record of how the servant of Abraham thus met Rebekah and was brought into the home of her family by the overruling providence of God we can see the guidance of God about which there is so much to be learned.

The conduct of the servant is very meaningful. The humility and thanksgiving of this man is notable, as is also his diligence. He did not waste any time in stating his mission. He told the parents of his prayer for guidance, of the sign he had asked from God, and of the way his prayer had been answered. Her parents left the decision of going to Isaac to be his bride with Rebekah; and she said, "I will go." Her parents wanted her to stay for at least ten more days, but the servant said, "Hinder me not, seeing the Lord hath prospered my way; send me away that I may go to my master." This is an important lesson for anyone becoming a Christian. It is a temptation upon hearing the call of God to hesitate, because answering His call will involve separation. But it is important that men freely respond promptly to God's call.

There is yet more to be learned in this account. Abraham's desire was to find a bride for his son. God desires to seek and to save souls. God sends evangelists with precious gifts of eternal blessing offered to all who will respond. Those who would be numbered among the "bride of Christ" must accept the call to come, and leave all else immediately to meet the Bridegroom. So it was with Rebekah, and so it must be with believers.

The Book of Genesis is largely composed of the biographies of great men of faith. It is common to hear of Abraham, Isaac, and Jacob. Of these three the impression is gained that Abraham and Jacob were the great men and that Isaac was less important, less favored of God. Abraham was the great man of faith, who was known as the "friend of God." Jacob, whose name was changed to Israel, was a prince of God, because of his power in prevailing prayer. There is nothing exceptional about the life of Isaac. He may be seen as a plain between two mountain peaks, Abraham and Jacob. He was notable for his wisdom. He was actually a great man.

> Then Isaac sowed in that land, and received in the same year an hundredfold: and the Lord blessed him. And the man waxed great, and went forward, and grew until he became very great: For he had possession of flocks, and possession of herds, and great store of servants: and the Philistines envied him (26:12-14).

Isaac had the problem of any young person who is the son of a prominent father. Abraham was great, capable, and successful. Isaac was wise. He walked in the footsteps of his father Abraham. His father was great, so Isaac did things as his father had done them.

> And Isaac digged again the wells of water, which they had digged in the days of Abraham his father; for the Philistines had stopped them after the death of Abraham: and he called their names after the names by which his father had called them (26:18).

The Philistines plugged up those wells; Isaac came along and restored them. Here is a profound lesson for young believers. Water is scarce in that arid land, and since Abraham had found an underground source of water, Isaac was smart enough to dig there.

The Holy Bible has been considered the Word of God for

generations. There is an enemy who has infiltrated the churches and has tried to obscure the power of the Word. Critics of the Bible have handled it in such a way as to stop the water coming into the well. So what should be done? Turn to the Bible again and look to God. Disregarding the critics, open the Bible and read it. For centuries no one in the churches doubted the doctrine of the virgin birth. The Bible taught it, Christians believed it, and every time the Apostles' Creed was recited, this truth was confessed. Present-day Philistines have cluttered this up with skeptical unbiblical unbelief and false arguments. What should be done today? Christians should remember the words of Gabriel, who said, "With God nothing is impossible," and reaffirm their faith in the virgin birth. The Bible tells us about the miracles that Jesus performed; Christians have believed them as they were written. Today scientific ideas are being offered implying that miracles are impossible. This hinders the flow of the water of life from the Bible. What shall be done? Look to God as other Christians have done and believe. The Bible speaks of salvation, of souls being saved through Christ's atoning death on Calvary. The "Philistines" today have come with psychology and social sciences and have so cluttered up our thinking that the word *saved* has been largely discredited. What should be done? Look at those whose lives have been changed by the Gospel and believe the Gospel. Not only should the wells our fathers digged be reopened, but the same language should be used. Once again Christians should talk about "saved by the blood," "there is power in the blood," and "the blood of Jesus Christ cleanseth from all sin." Christians today should use the words their forefathers used and mean them with all their hearts. Isaac digged again the wells of water that Abraham his father digged and called them by the names that Abraham his father had called them.

Chapter Eighteen

ESAU

(Genesis 25-27)

A popular notion is that a person is what he is because of his environment. So it follows that if the community is improved the people who live there will be improved. Some time ago all America was profoundly affected by a famous defense argument that was used during the trial for a brutal, senseless murder. A notorious lawyer, counsel for the defense, in an impassioned, brilliant plea, claimed that society was guilty, not his clients. He so influenced the jury that his clients escaped the death penalty which was their due according to the law. No doubt environment does have some effect, but too much weight should not be attached to this fact. Circumstances no doubt do alter cases but they do not settle them, and it is doubtful if they are ever the deciding factor in the prevention or the execution of a crime.

It is a human trait to blame circumstances for what happens. How often a youngster comes home and explains his misbehavior by saying, "Everybody else was doing it too." I have heard a father say at such a time, "If everybody jumped off a bridge, would you do it?" Blaming others for our misdeeds merely shows our reluctance to face unpleasant facts, causing us to bring in excuses and more excuses. This accounts for what Adam said when he had broken God's commandment (Gen. 3:12). When Aaron, influenced by the children of Israel, made a golden calf for their worship, he was called to account for his action by Moses. In his explanation Aaron told Moses that the people had brought their gold to him because they remembered the idols of Egypt and wanted an image to worship. He admitted that he had thrown the gold into the melting pot "and there came out this calf." In other words: "Don't blame me!"

I remember when a number of farmers were discussing this very subject. "Would a man act the way he does because of where he is?" They referred to an old English saying that has a bald, almost ruthless, candor in what it expresses: "You can't make a silk purse out of a sow's ear." They felt that in the attempt to improve people, much time and money has been spent in vain in trying to renovate whole communities. After repeated failures to change people by changing their environment this conclusion seems justified: "You can get a family out of the slums easily enough, but you can't get the slum out of the family so easily." This is to say again that although environment does make some difference, it does not take the place of responsibility.

The significance of environment can be seen in nature and history. A lily can grow in a swamp. On the same hillside oak trees and maple trees can grow. The rain and sunshine does not vary for each tree. The oak tree is there because of an acorn, and the apple tree is there because of an apple seed, according to the laws of nature. Cain and Abel had the same parents. They lived in the same surroundings, but they were different. Noah had three sons, but two of them differed from the third one. In our continuing study of the Book of Genesis, we come now to the classic example of the twins: Esau and Jacob. Their parents were Isaac and Rebekah. Their environment was certainly the same for each, and yet there was a personal difference between these brothers.

"Was not Esau Jacob's brother? saith the Lord: yet I loved Jacob, and I hated Esau" (Mal. 1:2-3). Paul refers to this in his letter to the Romans: "As it is written, Jacob have I loved, but Esau have I hated." What accounts for this difference in the attitude of God? The answer here, as in the case of Cain and Abel, must be that God looks into the heart.

And the boys grew: and Esau was a cunning hunter, a man of the field; and Jacob was a plain man, dwelling in tents. And Isaac loved Esau, because he did eat of his venison: but Rebekah loved Jacob. And Jacob sod pottage: and Esau came from the field, and he was faint: And Esau said to Jacob, Feed me, I pray thee, with that same red pottage; for I am faint: therefore was his name called Edom. And Jacob said, Sell me this day thy birthright. And Esau said, Behold, I am at the point to die: and what profit shall this birthright do to me? And Jacob said, Swear to me this day; and he sware unto him: and he sold his birthright unto Jacob. Then Jacob gave Esau bread and pottage of lentiles; and he did eat and drink, and rose up, and went his way: thus Esau despised his birthright (Gen. 25:27-34).

The truth in this situation seems quite obvious. Jacob had come in from his work in the fields and prepared his food. Esau had not prepared anything, but when he came by he wanted the food Jacob had prepared. Jacob wanted it too, which is why he had cooked it. When Esau asked for the food, Jacob offered to sell it to him for his birthright. Esau said, "What good is my birthright to me if I die of hunger?" So he agreed to the trade. This incident points up the difference between the two brothers.

In giving his birthright for something to eat, Esau belittled his birthright. God does not tolerate a man who will give up blessing from God for a moment's satisfaction. "And Esau have I hated." God hates anyone that will exchange a great benefit for the small gratification of a moment. Such a person cannot prosper with God. This truth is profoundly relevant today. It is the person who is willing to give up some temporary immediate pleasure in order to gain eternal, everlasting benefit who will receive the blessing of God. "Jacob have I loved." All through the story of Jacob it is recorded that above all else he wanted to have the blessing of God.

Esau and Jacob both knew that the promise of God to bless Abraham and their father Isaac would continue on from father to son in their family. God had said, "In Isaac shall thy seed be called." When Rebekah bore twins, before they were born, she had been told that "the elder shall serve the younger." The name Jacob literally translated means "Heel grabber." This is because when the children were born Esau was born first but Jacob's hand clutched Esau's heel. This was suggestive of Jacob's attitude in later life. The idea could be seen if two boys were climbing a ladder and the second boy reached up and grabbed the first one by the heel to hold him back. In the Hebrew language there is an expression referring to someone who takes advantage of another. In such a case they would say the one is trying to "Jacob" the other. The Bible does not tell us that the brothers knew of the prophecy that the older would serve the younger, but undoubtedly both knew of the blessing God had promised their father. Certainly Jacob sought the blessing of God.

In the course of time Esau felt great bitterness toward Jacob, because he felt that Jacob had cheated him out of his birthright. It may be true that the deal was not really a fair trade, even though Esau had agreed to the transaction of his own free will. It would seem that since God had promised the first place to the younger, Jacob need not have connived to get the birthright from Esau. Later we read of another incident in which Jacob again schemed to make sure he would get the blessing. This time his mother Rebekah overheard Isaac talking to Esau, telling him to go hunting for deer and prepare venison such as Isaac liked. On hearing this, Rebekah called to Jacob and told him what she had overheard. She asked him to fetch her two kids which she would prepare as savory meat. Then he was to take the meat to Isaac that he might receive Esau's blessing. Jacob was fearful that his father would discover such deception: "I shall seem to him as a deceiver; and I shall bring a curse upon me, and not a blessing." But his mother urged him, saying, " Upon me be thy curse, my son; only obey my voice, and go fetch me them." To complete the deception she brought Esau's clothes for Jacob to wear, and put the skins of the kids of the goats upon his hands and upon the smooth of his neck, because Esau was "a hairy man," and Jacob was "a smooth man." Isaac had some doubts when he heard Jacob's voice, but these were dispelled when he felt his hands and smelled the smell of the field upon the clothes. "And he discerned him not, because his hands were hairy, as his brother Esau's hands: so he blessed him." From here on the story speaks of Esau's grief and anger, and his hatred for Jacob when he discovered that his brother had by deceit received the blessing.

This deception of Isaac reveals much about the man Jacob. Isaac was in no way responsible for what had happened. This incident shows that an honest man can be deceived. But it shows about Jacob that he would do anything to get the blessing of God. The life of Jacob is an amazing example of the grace of God. In spite of Jacob's underhanded dealings, God later blessed him and used him. Before the twins were born Rebekah had been told that the older would serve the younger. Instead of waiting for the Lord to bring this to pass, she took things into her own hands and caused Jacob to deceive his father. We read that Rebekah loved Jacob and so she sent him away to escape from the wrath of Esau. She never saw Jacob again. It is natural to feel sorry for Esau. His story attracts popular sympathy, but the truth is that he was actually unworthy. He realized too late what he had lost, for "he cried with a great and exceeding bitter cry, and said unto his father, Bless me, even me also, O my father . . . Hast thou but one blessing, my father?" The record shows Isaac did have a lesser blessing for Esau. But Isaac could not reverse or recall the blessing which Jacob had received. This is a sobering thought: "Can blessing be forfeited? Can I lose the blessing of God?" This incident would teach this is true only when I am ready to give up the greater for the lesser.

Chapter Nineteen

JACOB

(Genesis 25-31)

The story of Jacob continues through chapter 28. His conduct so far has shown him to be a grasping person who wanted what was good for him. At the same time his deep rooted desire for the blessing of God is something to be appreciated. Jacob was forty years of age at the time when he left his home. That may seem old to us, but when we remember that the expected life span in those days was one hundred and twenty years he would be like a young man of twenty-two or twenty-three years of age in our day. On his first night away from home Jacob had a most amazing experience.

And Jacob went out from Beersheba, and went toward Haran. And he lighted upon a certain place, and tarried there all night, because the sun was set; and he took of the stones of that place, and put them for his pillows, and lay down in that place to sleep. And he dreamed, and behold a ladder set up on the earth, and the top of it reached to heaven: and behold the angels of God ascending and descending on it. And, behold, the Lord stood above it, and said, I am the Lord God of Abraham thy father, and the God of Isaac: the land whereon thou liest, to thee will I give it, and to thy seed; And thy seed shall be as the dust of the earth, and thou shalt spread abroad to the west, and to the east, and to the north, and to the south: and in thee and in thy seed shall all the families of the earth be blessed. And, behold, I am with thee, and will keep thee in all places whither thou goest, and will bring thee again into this land; for I will not leave thee, until I have done that which I have spoken to thee of (Gen. 28:10-15).

In this vision or dream he was given a great promise. The word *ladder* that we find here is not the best translation of the Hebrew word, which implies "ascending steps" something like a staircase. The important thing is that this was a means of communication between earth and heaven.

When Jacob saw this ladder reaching from this earth to heaven, he realized the reality of heaven, and that everything that takes place on this earth matters in heaven. The angels of God "ascending and descending" this staircase point to the real communication which takes place between earth and heaven. The vision shows there is actually an interaction between the two, between earth and heaven, and over it all is God, who created both. This God, who is Creator of all, spoke the words of promise and blessing to Jacob.

> And Jacob awaked out of his sleep, and he said, Surely the Lord is in this place; and I knew it not. And he was afraid, and said, How dreadful is this place! this is none other but the house of God, and this is the gate of heaven. And Jacob rose up early in the morning, and took the stone that he had put for his pillows, and set it up for a pillar, and poured oil upon the top of it. And he called the name of that place Bethel: but the name of that city was called Luz at the first (28:16-19).

When he said, "How dreadful is this place," he meant "How overwhelming and awesome is this place." He felt that he was in the presence of God and he bowed to the ground and worshiped.

> And Jacob vowed a vow, saying, If God will be with me, and will keep me in this way that I go, and will give me bread to eat, and raiment to put on, so that I come again to my father's house in peace; then shall the Lord be my God: And this stone which I have set for a pillar, shall be God's house: and of all that thou shalt give me I will surely give the tenth unto thee (28:20-22).

When Jacob says, "If God will be with me," he is not expressing a doubt. It is more like saying, "Since God will be with me." For instance we could say to a mother, "If that's your child, take care of it." What we really mean is "Since that is your child." There is no doubt in Jacob's mind. He had been given this vision and had heard the promise of God. He was ready to put all his trust in Him, and to put Him first above all else. He was prepared to give God his full allegiance.

There is no good reason for thinking that Jacob was bargaining with God. By giving one-tenth he recognized that God was giving him everything. It is like our worship of God. We worship God at all times, but we set aside Sunday for special worship services. That is one day in seven. When we turn to God on Sunday we are not to turn away from Him during the following days of the week, but rather we worship Him at all times. So it is with the tithe. We receive all we have from God and then we set aside one tenth to show it. By the way, the tithe is not for God. He does not need the money. I need to give it for my own soul's sake. This is the principle of tithing, and Jacob recognized this.

After this dream and the promises of God to encourage him, Jacob went on his journey and came into the land of the people of the East. He stopped at a well and inquired of some men he met there about his mother's brother Laban. They knew him well, but before he could inquire further, Laban's daughter Rachel came to the well to water her sheep. Jacob watered them for her and then told her who he was. When Rachel heard that he was Rebekah's son, she ran to tell her father about him.

> And it came to pass, when Laban heard the tidings of Jacob his sister's son, that he ran to meet him, and embraced him, and kissed him, and brought him to his house. And he told Laban all these things (29:13).

Jacob told Laban of the reason for his coming and Laban invited him to stay in his home. No doubt Jacob rendered valuable service to Laban, because after a month had passed Laban asked Jacob to name his wages and to continue working for him. Because Jacob loved Rachel he said, "I will serve thee seven years, for Rachel thy younger daughter." This arrangement was agreed upon; "and Jacob served seven years for Rachel; and they seemed unto him but a few days, for the love he had to her."

In the wedding ceremony it was the custom that a bride would wear a veil over her face. So when the seven years were ended and Jacob came for his bride, it was an easy thing for Laban to deceive him and give him his older daughter in marriage. Jacob was shocked and complained to Laban:

> And it came to pass, that in the morning, behold, it was Leah: and he said to Laban, What is this thou hast done unto me? did not I serve with thee for Rachel? wherefore then hast thou beguiled me? (29:25).

Laban explained that in his country it was the custom to marry the older daughter off first. Then Jacob agreed to work seven more years for Rachel.

In the fourteen years that Jacob worked for Rachel, Laban tried to cheat him again and again. It is written that he changed Jacob's wages ten times. After Rachel's son Joseph was born, Jacob said unto Laban, "Send me away, that I may go unto mine own place, and to my country." Laban urged Jacob to stay, "For I have learned by experience that the Lord hath blessed me for thy sake." Jacob consented to stay on. For his wages he was to receive cattle and sheep. As the months passed into years and his flocks and herds increased, Laban and his sons resented Jacob's wealth and began to persecute him. The Word of the Lord then came to him: "And the Lord said unto Jacob, Return unto the land of thy fathers, and to thy kindred; and I will be with thee" (31:3). Jacob called Rachel and Leah to the field and said, "And ye know that with all my power I have served your father. And your father hath deceived me, and changed my wages ten times; but God suffered him not to hurt me" (31:6-7). Both Rachel and Leah understood how their father had treated Jacob and they were ready to go with him to his own country.

Jacob gathered his flocks and cattle and camels and servants and set his children and his wives on camels, as he started on his journey to Canaan. He set out from a ranch which was far from the home place, while it was still night, because he wanted no trouble with Laban, the Syrian. "And it was told Laban on the third day that Jacob was fled" (31:22). Laban at once gathered together his men and pursued after Jacob to make trouble for him, but God came to him in a dream and warned him to do Jacob no harm. When Laban caught up with Jacob, he said that God had spoken to him, and warned him to treat Jacob well. Then he accused Jacob of having stolen his idols before leaving. Jacob had no way of knowing that Rachel had taken them and hidden them in the trappings of her camel and was sitting on them. So he told Laban to search for them. Laban and his men searched Jacob's and Leah's and Rachel's tents without finding even a trace of them.

Jacob resented Laban's suspicions and protested his innocence.

> And Jacob was wroth, and chode with Laban: and Jacob answered and said to Laban, What is my trespass? what is my sin, that thou hast so hotly pursued after me? Whereas thou hast searched all my stuff, what hast thou found of all thy household stuff? set it here before my brethren and thy brethren, that they may judge betwixt us both. This twenty years have I been with thee; thy ewes and thy she goats have not cast their young, and the rams of thy flock have I not eaten. That which was torn of beasts I brought not unto thee; I bare the loss of it; of my hand didst thou require it, whether stolen by day, or stolen by night. Thus I was; in the day the drought consumed me, and the frost by night; and my sleep departed from mine eyes. Thus have I been twenty years in thy house; I served thee fourteen years for thy two daughters, and six years for thy cattle: and thou hast changed my wages ten times. Except the God of my father, the God of Abraham, and the fear of Isaac, had been with me, surely thou hadst sent me away now empty. God hath seen mine affliction and the labour of my hands, and rebuked thee yesternight (31:36-42).

Then Laban, feeling that he had wronged Jacob, made a covenant with him. They erected a pillar of stone for a remembrance, and Laban and his men remained there overnight and then took leave of his daughters and their children.

Rachel's theft of her father's idols indicates a common tendency. Often when a person becomes a Christian he may bring along ideas that belong to his home or to the community he grew up in. Many of us are guilty of this very thing. We take with us a lot of ideas into our Christian life which would be better left behind, because they can only hamper our walk with the Lord. This example of Rachel should cause all of us to do some soul-searching and to put away all that does not belong to a life of faith.

Chapter Twenty

ISRAEL

(Genesis 32-36)

After taking his departure from Laban, Jacob traveled on with his family and all his livestock. When he neared his native land he was beset by the fear that Esau his brother, who had threatened his life twenty years before, might still make his threat good. So he sent messengers before him to Esau.

> And he commanded them, saying, Thus shall ye speak unto my lord Esau; Thy servant Jacob saith thus, I have sojourned with Laban, and stayed there until now: And I have oxen, and asses, flocks, and menservants, and womenservants: and I have sent to tell my lord, that I may find grace in thy sight. And the messengers returned to Jacob, saying, We came to thy brother Esau, and also he cometh to meet thee, and four hundred men with him. Then Jacob was greatly afraid and distressed: and he divided the people that was with him, and the flocks, and herds, and the camels, into two bands; And said, If Esau come to the one company, and smite it, then the other company which is left shall escape (Gen. 32:4-8).

After he had carried out this plan and had done all he knew to do, Jacob turned to God in prayer and supplication. In his prayer it seems that he is calling on God on the basis of His promise. It was God who had blessed him while he was serving Laban, and it was God who had told him to return to the land of Canaan.

> And Jacob said, O God of my father Abraham, and God of my father Isaac, the Lord which saidst unto me, Return unto thy country, and to thy kindred, and I will deal well

with thee: I am not worthy of the least of all the mercies, and of all the truth, which thou hast shewed unto thy servant; for with my staff I passed over this Jordan; and now I am become two bands. Deliver me, I pray thee, from the hand of my brother, from the hand of Esau: for I fear him, lest he will come and smite me, and the mother with the children. And thou saidst, I will surely do thee good, and make thy seed as the sand of the sea, which cannot be numbered for multitude (32:9-12).

Jacob knew that he was in great danger and he called upon God as any believer would pray in like circumstances: "Lord, help me. Be merciful to me."

Though he was asking God to help him, Jacob showed his personal cleverness in the very astute way in which he dealt with his brother.

And he lodged there that same night; and took of that which came to his hand a present for Esau his brother; Two hundred she goats, and twenty he goats, two hundred ewes, and twenty rams, thirty milch camels with their colts, forty kine, and ten bulls, twenty she asses, and ten foals. And he delivered them into the hand of his servants, every drove by themselves; and said unto his servants, Pass over before me, and put a space betwixt drove and drove. And he commanded the foremost, saying, When Esau my brother meeteth thee, and asketh thee, saying, Whose art thou? and whither goest thou? and whose are these before thee? Then thou shalt say, They be thy servant Jacob's; it is a present sent unto my lord Esau: and, behold, also he is behind us. And so commanded he the second, and the third, and all that followed the droves, saying, On this manner shall ye speak unto Esau, when ye find him. And say ye moreover, Behold, thy servant Jacob is behind us. For he said, I will appease him with the present that goeth before me, and afterward I will see his face; peradventure he will accept of me. So went the present over before him: and himself lodged that night in the company (32:13-21).

Today we would call such an approach "applied psychology." This is an example of human wit and cleverness. It was actually the wisest thing he could do, and Jacob was smart enough to know that sooner or later a day of reckoning must come and consequences must be faced. He knew that he could never handle this situation by himself and yet he did what he could.

Jacob believed in God. It is wonderful to realize that a man need not be good or strong or even above reproach to be able to count on the blessing of God if he believes in Him. God is gracious and merciful. He waits for a humble, contrite heart which turns to Him seeking His divine blessing. So it can be with anybody. When a storm approaches and I seek shelter, how wonderful to find a rocky cave where I will be safe and secure from the storm. The shelter is not there because of any goodness on my part: it is there by the providence of God. He is my shelter and my refuge in any storm. Salvation is by His grace. Knowledge of my own sinfulness and unworthiness must never stand in my way when I need a Savior. He came for the very purpose of seeking and saving sinners. When I know my own weakness, then His strength will see me through.

The record goes on to reveal the very heart of Jacob's experience: "Jacob was left alone." Face to face with his peril this man was alone. Then the account goes on to report: "And there wrestled a man with him until the breaking of the day." Bible students have felt this was an angel who came as a messenger. So far as Jacob was concerned, it was a man he wrestled with until the break of day. Jacob was doing all he could but he was not able to overcome the man. But even so, the man was not able to overcome Jacob because he persisted in holding on. At the break of day Jacob was still desperately hanging on to the man. It was then that the messenger crippled Jacob: "and the hollow of Jacob's thigh was out of joint," and yet he would not let go. Jacob still clung to the man. When the messenger indicated he wanted to depart, Jacob cried out, "I will not let thee go, except thou bless me."

Before the angel left, he asked, "What is thy name? And he said, Jacob." But in God's sight Jacob was now ready for a new name.

> And he said, Thy name shall be called no more Jacob, but Israel: for as a prince hast thou power with God and with men, and hast prevailed (32:28).

And he blessed him there. Thus Jacob received great spiritual blessing, though not without physical suffering. Jacob limped when he walked from that day on, having been humbled by God. Yet he had received so very, very much. He had been given a new name which in itself was a promise and a benediction, "For as a prince hast thou power with God and with men, and hast prevailed."

The believer can read about Jacob and rejoice in the assurance that God has not changed. He is ever ready to hear when His people call on Him. He is a God of grace and mercy and compassion. It is written that "He is touched with all the feelings of our infirmities." It is wonderful to remember God is no respecter of persons: anyone may come and partake of His salvation, which He offers as a free gift. Just as it is true that as long as he lived in this world Jacob limped and still had to endure many disappointments, even so it is also true in the lives of Christians that they may have sorrow and loss even after they accept Christ.

Christians may lose a beloved child and even begin to have misgivings about the power of prayer, but they need to remember this is the time to hang on to God, who will give strength to endure and faith to trust Him. When the Christian knows this from the bottom of his heart, he will bless God's name even in ills and in sorrows.

Some Christians are distressed because of the animosity which some people feel toward them for no other reason than that they represent the Lord. Any who are troubled with this kind of a situation can be comforted to know they can follow in some small measure their Lord's example. Jesus of Nazareth was rejected and eventually killed by the very people He came to save.

Undeserved animosity and even hatred without cause was certainly exemplified in the life of Joseph. Joseph was Rachel's firstborn, and he was greatly beloved by his father. We know how very much Jacob loved Rachel, so this may have been one reason why he loved her son. When Joseph was seventeen years of age, he was an obedient son. He was reliable and respectful toward his father and we find that he displayed high integrity in his personal conduct. He was ready to help and to serve others. Altogether Joseph was a superior person, and this caused his brothers to hate him. It was also true that he received favorable recognition. Rewarding someone who does well should not be criticized. It is a common fact that outstanding students in school receive recognition. Being noted for doing well can cause certain reactions. There is the classic case of Cain and Abel. When God had respect unto Abel's offering, Cain was angry. This was not Abel's fault, but it happened to him nevertheless. Even today when Christians really seek to serve God, when they want to be sincere and humble and reverent, as they study His Word and pray, there will be people who will oppose and dislike them. This sort of thing has happened all through history, down to the present day. So it was with Joseph when his brothers were envious of him, even though he had done nothing to deserve this.

Hatred of the rich is also very common among mankind. People who are rich and prominent and have position and power are often hated. Such hatred can actually be grounded in self-love. A man's personal egotism can't bear to see someone else better off than himself. This type of egotism with its envy and jealousies is the most common source for trouble between people. Joseph certainly had to face this sort of thing. But there was something else about Joseph which did not endear him to his brothers. Joseph knew that some day he would be the most important person in his family. He knew this when he was just a teen-ager because of his dreams, and he spoke of it quite openly. He was probably neither proud nor vain, but rather spoke of his dreams in an interested, honest way. But this provoked his brothers to greater jealousy and envy and hostility.

It is written, "A man's foes shall be they of his own household." There are young Christians whose family makes fun of them. They resent the fact that someone in their own family circle is reading the Bible and praying. It is good to remember that such people can be changed by the transforming grace and power of God. Jacob, who in his youth had been conniving and all for self, was changed when he met God face to face. It is possible for a man's whole personality and character to change, but only by the grace of God. A man can receive a totally new outlook on things. His thoughts will no longer revolve around self and his immediate circumstances. His eyes will be lifted up to higher levels and higher ambitions. He will behold the King in all His beauty, and his soul will be filled with praise and thanksgiving. Such a man will also face the future with new aspirations and expectations when he is called to a significant place of service by the Lord. When David knew that he was to become king over Israel, his whole outlook changed. His thoughts turned to God in psalms of praise and trust. When he was anointed by Samuel while a teen-ager, he acquired new values and new ambitions. In the New Testament, in 2 Corinthians 5:17, we read these meaningful words: "If any man be in Christ, he is a new creature: old things are passed away; behold, all things are become new." We notice here that it is the "old things" which are passed away. This verse does not only refer to the ego and the old nature. It is the individual himself who "becomes new" in his thinking and in his attitude when he establishes a connection and a relationship with God. We are reminded of the occasion when our Lord said to Peter, "Thou art called Simon; thou shalt be called Peter." The word *Simon* refers to "sand," and the word *Peter* means "rock." A house built upon sand will give way; a rock stands fast throughout every storm. Peter, whose old nature had much that was impetuous and unstable about it, changed after the Lord dealt with him. He became steadfast and faithful even unto death. I may try to do the best I can, but I will never succeed until I come face to face with God. Then, as in the case of Jacob and Peter, something can actually happen to me. I will no longer seek my own, but I will seek to do God's will. All this can be felt in the story of Joseph and his brethren.

Chapter Twenty-one

JOSEPH IN TROUBLE

(Genesis 37-39)

As a lad Joseph experienced two strange dreams. In his first dream he beheld his brothers' sheaves which they were binding in the field, making obeisance to his sheaf. In his second dream, the sun and the moon and eleven stars made obeisance to him. These dreams seemed to predict that Joseph would be the most prominent member of the family. Because of this his brothers hated him all the more. When they saw him afar off, coming to learn of their affairs for his father, they "conspired against him to slay him."

> And they said one to another, Behold, this dreamer cometh. Come now therefore, and let us slay him, and cast him into some pit, and we will say, Some evil beast hath devoured him: and we shall see what will become of his dreams (Gen. 37:19-20).

Reuben, the oldest of the brothers, would not agree to such a thing.

> And Reuben said unto them, Shed no blood, but cast him into this pit that is in the wilderness, and lay no hand upon him; that he might rid him out of their hands, to deliver him to his father again (37:22).

So when Reuben left they stripped Joseph of his coat of many colors and cast him into the pit.

Looking toward the east his brethren saw a caravan of merchants approaching, and Judah said, "Come, and let us sell him to the Ishmaelites." So they lifted Joseph out of the pit and sold him for twenty pieces of silver.

And they took Joseph's coat, and killed a kid of the goats, and dipped the coat in the blood; And they sent the coat of many colours, and they brought it to their father; and said, This have we found: know now whether it be thy son's coat or no. And he knew it, and said, It is my son's coat; an evil beast hath devoured him; Joseph is without doubt rent in pieces. And Jacob rent his clothes, and put sackcloth upon his loins, and mourned for his son many days (37:31-34).

So the result was that Joseph was taken into Egypt. "And the Midianites sold him into Egypt unto Potiphar, an officer of Pharaoh's, and captain of the guard."

This is the Bible account of the heartless cruelty of Joseph's brothers and of his escape from death. Some questions arise which can be considered with profit. Should Joseph have reported to his father what his brothers were doing? ". . . and Joseph brought unto his father their evil report." Obviously Joseph saw that some of his brothers were dealing deceitfully, and told Jacob of it. Does a man have a responsibility to report wrongdoing when he sees it? If we see a felony committed, should we hold our peace? Does reporting a felony make us informers? And should that be held against us? When we are expected to make a report on someone's dishonesty, can we in good conscience cover up dishonesty for fear of retribution? Should Jacob have sent Joseph to check up on his brothers? Why not? After all Jacob had the overall responsibility, and he would need to know how things were being handled. He had to send someone who was honest and dependable, and so it seems right and natural that he would send Joseph. Another question that is frequently asked is, "Did Jacob not realize that giving Joseph a coat of many colors would cause envy among his other sons and make Joseph obnoxious to them?" What should have been done in a case like this? Shall we refrain from expressing appreciation of the good because we fear to offend the bad? As this whole situation is considered there seems to be no valid reason why Jacob should not show his appreciation for Joseph with a gift of a coat of many colors. No doubt this would bring Joseph to the attention of everyone, but telling the truth would do this for anybody.

No doubt Joseph may have been quite unaware that his brothers hated him so bitterly. A humble person dreaming that he would become prominent and powerful might speak of it to his family because it was such a strange and exciting dream. After all Joseph was seventeen years of age, and dreams of this nature could surprise and impress him, so that he would want to share them with his family. Actually these dreams of his were valid. They predicted what would happen later in his life. This gives pause for thought. God can speak in dreams. There are several examples of this in the Bible.

In these "last days" God speaks to all who will hear through His Son, but this does not rule out the possibility that He might speak in dreams even today. When this happens, there may be no doubt in the heart and mind of such a person that God has a message for him.

Some feel that Joseph was honorable and trustworthy in all his ways because of prenatal influence. It is written that Jacob loved Rachel very deeply, and psychologists say that a child born of a marriage where true love is involved has a better opportunity of having a well-balanced personality. Apparently love between parents has a definite effect upon the child. On the other hand, it is possible that Cain was greatly beloved because he was the firstborn son of Adam and Eve. Noah may have loved every one of his sons, but the record is clear that one was unworthy. This whole idea of prenatal influence remains uncertain and obscure.

In the record of Joseph the serious truth is revealed that a person who is obedient to God will suffer persecution. Paul writing to Timothy speaks of this very thing. "All that will live godly in Christ Jesus shall suffer persecution." "Godly" simply means that a person would be obedient to God. In the final analysis it is God's strength and God's grace which produce a "godly" life. No man in himself is good enough or strong or wise enough to live in the will of God without His guiding Spirit and enabling grace. John, in referring to Cain, writes:

> And wherefore slew he him? Because his own works were
> evil, and his brother's righteous. Marvel not, my brethren,
> if the world hate you (1 John 3:12-13).

Such Scripture helps Christians to understand their own
experiences which try the soul.

It is true for all who have wondered about walking with
the Lord that as far as this world is concerned, they need
not expect preferential treatment. As a matter of fact it is
more than likely they will find that when they become
disciples of our Lord they will be disliked and avoided.
Peter writes:

> For this is thankworthy, if a man for conscience toward
> God endure grief, suffering wrongfully. For what glory
> is it, if, when ye be buffeted for your faults, ye shall take
> it patiently? but if, when ye do well, and suffer for it, ye
> take it patiently, this is acceptable with God (1 Pet. 2:19-
> 20).

What a privilege it is to bear some comparatively small
distress and humiliation for His name's sake! Blessed are all
who have an opportunity to so endure, because they are
obedient to the Lord and are found to be trustworthy in
His sight.

In the Old Testament there are a number of men of God
whose lives reflected no evil. Joseph is a shining example
of someone who from his earliest youth walked uprightly
and pleasingly to God. Through no fault of his own, he
aroused hostility and envy, and even active hatred among
his brothers. Without the ending of this story which began
with so much violence, this portion of God's Word would
seem to illustrate a prime example of injustice. But the
record goes on to show that God had His hand in all that
happened and that He was able to bring good out of evil.
God used Joseph in Egypt for a far-reaching and most important divine plan for the good of His people.

Everything in the life of Joseph so carefully recorded in
the Book of Genesis is there not only that we should come
to know Joseph himself, but primarily for our learning. It
is to encourage believers to live in this world by putting
their trust in God.

In chapter 39 there is recorded a rather long account of a sordid affair in which Potiphar's wife tried to seduce Joseph and failed because of Joseph's steadfast refusal to sin against God. In her anger the woman falsely accused Joseph.

> And it came to pass, when his master heard the words of his wife, which she spake unto him, saying, After this manner did thy servant to me; that his wrath was kindled. And Joseph's master took him, and put him into the prison, a place where the king's prisoners were bound: and he was there in the prison (39:19-20).

The story shows that Joseph, although only a slave, was in a position of responsibility and trust. His master had put everything in his house into his care. Joseph accepted this position of trust not only from his master but from God. He understood this rightly. If he betrayed his master's trust in him, he knew that he would be sinning against God. This temptation came while he was attending to his daily round of duties.

Joseph withstood the woman day by day, but when pressure increased and she laid hands on him he fled. Joseph did not display proud self-confidence in the face of something which could be fatal. He was humble enough and wise enough to get out. Despite his wise efforts to avoid trouble, Joseph was falsely accused on the basis of false evidence. He was quite helpless to deny any wrongdoing because his garment was offered as evidence. Lies can include half-truths. There are people who are always ready to believe the worst and then to spread it to others. When this woman brought her accusations she referred slightingly to Joseph as "that Hebrew servant." This aroused a feeling of prejudice and inspired critical judgment in those who heard her. Joseph could do nothing about it, and he was judged guilty by Potiphar. As a result Joseph was thrown into prison in shame and disgrace. How utterly unfair and unjust to be cut off from any opportunity for vindication. Humanly speaking he was ruined. Now only God could help him.

Chapter Twenty-two

JOSEPH IN POWER

(Genesis 40-45)

There is much in the story of Joseph that corresponds to life today. In this record there is much to learn about the overruling providence of God. How often we miss the true meaning of life because we take things for granted and overlook the fact that everything comes from God. When we do well, we are so prone to take credit for ourselves. It is so easy to expect praise for what we have accomplished. But in the sight of God the praise of men is not valid. God looks upon the hearts of men. When Christ saw the widow cast two mites into the treasury He astonished His disciples by telling them that her gift was greater than the large amounts of money the rich had given. In the same way, God evaluates what we give and do, after He opens doors and presents opportunities for service.

The record shows that if Joseph had not been in prison he would not have met the butler from the court of Pharaoh. If God had not given Joseph the interpretation of the baker's and the butler's dreams, he would never have been called into the presence of the ruler of all Egypt.

Two of Pharaoh's chief servants offended him, and as a result had been cast into the same dungeon where Joseph was imprisoned. While in prison each of these men had a most disturbing dream. Joseph noticed their distress and asked them why they were sad and troubled. When they told him of their dreams Joseph said unto them, "Do not interpretations belong to God?" Then he proceeded to tell them the meaning of their dreams. The chief jailer had put Joseph into a place of responsibility because he was capable and trustworthy. He had conducted himself in such a way that the keeper of the prison had appointed him "trusty" over all the other prisoners. Having told the baker and the butler of the meaning of their dreams, he said to the butler, who would soon be restored to his position with Pharaoh:

> But think on me when it shall be well with thee, and shew kindness, I pray thee, unto me, and make mention of me unto Pharaoh, and bring me out of this house: for indeed I was stolen away out of the land of the Hebrews: and here also have I done nothing that they should put me into the dungeon (Gen. 40:14-15).

We can imagine how he awaited some news of deliverance, but the butler forgot all about Joseph for two long years. After that something happened in the providence of God that completely changed Joseph's life.

Pharaoh dreamed a dream so strange and somehow ominous that he called together all the magicians and wise men, and told them his dream; but none of them could interpret his dream. Then the butler bethought himself of Joseph. He told of his dream while in prison. "And there was there with us a young man, an Hebrew, servant to the captain of the guard . . . as he interpreted to us, so it was" (41:12-13). When Pharoah heard this, he hastily called for Joseph. He told Joseph of his dream which none could interpret: "And I have heard say of thee, that thou canst understand a dream to interpret it. And Joseph answered Pharaoh, saying, It is not in me: God shall give Pharaoh an answer of peace" (41:15-16). There is much to learn from Joseph in his encounter with the king. Joseph did not try to promote himself. He was humble, and he knew and made it known that his God was able to send and interpret dreams.

The hand of God was directing the events in Joseph's life all through his career. Joseph could not have saved himself when his brothers wanted to kill him. He could not have saved himself when Reuben suggested that they throw him into a pit instead. Even the brothers themselves did not know that the Ishmaelites would come along when they did. To them this might have seemed like a fortunate turn of events which gave them the opportunity to get rid of Joseph. But none of this was an accident; God had His hand in everything that happened. If Potiphar had not bought him for a slave, the rest of the story would not have occurred. All of this demonstrates that if a man will trust God, He will set a train of events into motion that will honor faith and bring His will to pass. Even the time Joseph spent in prison turned to his benefit. How else could he have met the butler of Pharaoh? Those extra two years may seem cruel but it was after that time that Pharaoh dreamed and needed him. God's timing may be obscure to us as events unfold, but we can be sure that God makes no mistakes. Surely Joseph did not expect to be made the prime minister of Egypt. Taking all into consideration, it must be concluded that this was God's plan for Joseph. This was what Joseph had been born to do.

Again and again the overruling power of God can be seen in the lives of those who believe His promises and trust Him to fulfill them. In the providence and sovereignty of God, Joseph was much more than the prime minister of Egypt. He became the deliverer of his own people and was called upon to act as judge over his brothers. Any judge should be fair. He should be intelligent. The purpose of a judge is to set out what is right and what is wrong. He must not let his personal feelings affect his decision no matter whom it involves. Neither personal relationships nor friendships should influence his verdict. This is one reason why parents find it so difficult to judge the actions of their children. Their love and affection for them blinds them to their duty. On the other hand, they find it easy to pass harsh judgment on those whom they dislike. This is never good. Joseph had every reason to deal harshly with his brothers. They had wanted to kill him and then had sold him as a slave.

Years had passed since that day, but it is written that when a famine stalked the land of Canaan, and was "over all the face of the earth," Jacob told his sons to go down into the land of Egypt to buy corn, "that we may live, and not die." Jacob kept Benjamin, Rachel's second son with him. He had lost Joseph and had mourned for him for many years. He could not bear to part with Benjamin, Joseph's brother, "lest peradventure mischief befall him."

His brothers did not realize they would be dealing with Joseph. "And the sons of Israel came to buy corn . . . but they knew him not." But as his brothers bowed before him seeking his favor, Joseph remembered the dreams he had dreamed. He planned to deal with them in a way which would prick their consciences and recall to their minds the brutal way in which they had treated him. He did not do this with any feeling of animosity, nor was he seeking retribution. Joseph knew that unless they faced the evil they had committed and repented, they would never really be free from the past. To do this he made himself speak roughly to them. He accused them of being spies. "And he put them all together into ward three days." That is to say that he put them into prison. At the end of three days he told them that one of them would have to stay behind, bound and imprisoned, until they returned with their youngest brother Benjamin, ostensibly to prove that the things they had told him about his family were true. The record tells the moving story of their remorse, and of Joseph's reaction to their words:

> And they said one to another, We are verily guilty concerning our brother, in that we saw the anguish of his soul, when he besought us, and we would not hear; therefore is this distress come upon us. And Reuben answered them, saying, Spake I not unto you, saying, Do not sin against the child; and ye would not hear? therefore, behold, also his blood is required. And they knew not that Joseph understood them; for he spake unto them by an interpreter. And he turned himself about from them, and wept; and returned to them again, and communed with them, and took from them Simeon, and bound him before their eyes (42:21-24).

Before they left with their sacks of grain, Joseph commanded that the money they had paid for it be returned to them. When one of the brothers opened his sack of grain,

"he espied the money" . . . and he told it to his brothers
and, "their heart failed them, and they were afraid, saying
one to another, What is this that God hath done unto us?"
In all their misfortune they saw the hand of God in their
affairs. Their feeling of guilt, which had been aroused by
Joseph, now increased. They felt that somehow this whole
thing which put them in jeopardy as thieves was punishment
for their past wickedness.

The famine increased in the land of Canaan. When all
the grain the brethren had brought out of Egypt was gone
and Jacob and his whole household were faced with starvation, he said to his sons, "Go again and buy us a little food."
Judah, acting as spokesman for the brothers, reminded his
father that they could never face the Lord of Egypt again
unless they were accompanied by their brother Benjamin.
But Jacob was afraid:

> And he said, My son shall not go down with you; for his
> brother is dead, and he is left alone: if mischief befall him
> by the way in the which ye go, then shall ye bring down
> my gray hairs with sorrow to the grave (42:38).

(It may be helpful to remember that Joseph and Benjamin
were the only two sons of Jacob's beloved wife, Rachel.)
As the days went by and the lack of corn grew more desperate, Judah said to his father:

> Send the lad with me, and we will arise and go; that we
> may live, and not die, both we, and thou, and also our
> little ones. I will be surety for him; of my hand shalt thou
> require him: if I bring him not unto thee, and set him
> before thee, then let me bear the blame for ever (43:8-9).

So Jacob with a heavy heart sent Benjamin along with
Judah and his brothers. He gave them twice the required
money to make up for the money that had been returned
to them in their bags.

The brothers left their sorrowful father and went down
into Egypt, "and stood before Joseph." When Joseph saw
his brother Benjamin, he was greatly moved and told his
chief steward to prepare a banquet and to take his brothers
to his home.

And the men were afraid, because they were brought into Joseph's house; and they said, Because of the money that was returned in our sacks at the first time are we brought in; that he may seek occasion against us, and fall upon us, and take us for bondmen, and our asses (43:18).

It was utterly incredible to them that this great man of the realm would invite them to his home for any good purpose. Joseph observed their fear, but to spare them suffering at this time would be premature. They needed to be deeply humbled and tested. The brothers' dread of evil only increased when Joseph placed them at the table in order of their ages. Then Joseph had Benjamin served five times as much as the others. He waited for some sign of resentment at this, but there was none. After the meal Joseph dismissed all his brothers in order that they might return to their father and their families.

Early in the morning the brethren started out for Canaan not knowing that their money was again returned to them and that a silver cup had been placed in Benjamin's sack. They had not gone far when they realized that they were being pursued by Joseph's stewards. They stopped, fearful of what might happen, and were told that Joseph's silver cup was missing and that they were suspects. The brothers were so sure of their innocence that they invited a search of all their bags, and offered to stay and be Joseph's slaves if the silver cup were found in their possession. The Egyptians began a systematic search from the oldest to the youngest. When they opened Benjamin's sack, they found Joseph's silver cup. At this terrible discovery the brothers rent their clothes in anguish and, reloading their beasts of burden, returned to the city. The brothers were sure that their evil past was being punished, "God hath found out the iniquity of thy servants: behold, we are my lord's servants, both we, and he also with whom the cup is found." Joseph now told them that they were all free to go except for Benjamin, in whose sack the silver cup had been found.

Judah stepped forward and pleaded to be allowed to stay in Benjamin's place. He told Joseph that his father's heart would be broken if he lost his youngest son. When Joseph heard Judah, he needed no further proof of the tremendous change which had taken place in them. (He had the proof of their true repentance.) "And he wept aloud." Then he revealed himself to them.

> And Joseph said unto his brethren, Come near to me, I pray you. And they came near. And he said, I am Joseph your brother, whom ye sold into Egypt. Now therefore be not grieved, nor angry with yourselves, that ye sold me hither: for God did send me before you to preserve life (45:4-5).

Joseph explained how he would provide for them.

> And he fell upon his brother Benjamin's neck, and wept; and Benjamin wept upon his neck. Moreover he kissed all his brethren, and wept upon them: and after that his brethren talked with him (45:14-15).

After this Joseph went to Pharaoh and was given every help to bring his father and all his household to him in Egypt. Joseph interpreted everything that happened as the will of God. There is no hint of resentment, no thought of retaliation. We marvel as we read of the remarkable conduct of this man. Surely, only the grace of God could motivate the human heart in this way.

Chapter Twenty-three

JOSEPH IN TRIUMPH

(Genesis 45)

The amazing story of Joseph becomes increasingly impressive as it is studied. How I could wish and pray that my life might be as free from resentment and thoughts of retaliation as his was. How often it is true that when a person suffers injustice he becomes bitter and harsh. When we are wrongfully treated we are tempted to keep thinking about the person who has mistreated us until we convince ourselves that it is only right that we should pay him back for the wrong done to us. When we permit such an attitude to dominate our thinking, we will actually harm ourselves more than anyone else. It could affect my whole personality and cause me to become truculent and blindly opposed to everyone and everything. I know that when I meet someone who is surly and sulky I feel inclined to avoid him. I feel that he should know of himself that if he has had trouble this is common to all men. A man who carries a chip on his shoulder will not be chosen to be in charge of others. When we consider the terrible injustice Joseph endured we would say that he had reason for bitterness and justifiable anger, but we find no evidence of this.

When we read that Potiphar entrusted all his affairs to Joseph, we may be sure that he was trustworthy and capable and courteous. When Potiphar's wife falsely accused him and he was unjustly condemned and put into prison, he certainly had reason to turn his face to the wall and his back to the world and become bitter and sulky. Instead of this we read that the chief jailer put the other prisoners under his supervision. In his dealings with the butler and the baker, we see him sympathetic and helpful. When he had an opportunity to take credit to himself for having interpreted their dreams, he gave God the honor due Him. When in the providence of God Joseph was given supreme authority in all of Egypt, he did not become proud. When his brothers knelt at his feet in humble request for food he was not arrogant or vengeful. Such conduct on his part reveals Joseph's wonderful enduring inner strength, which carried him through every tragedy and through the succeeding honor and glory which came to him.

The secret source of Joseph's strength was that he believed in God. He believed beyond the shadow of a doubt that all which had happened had been in the gracious will of God. He believed that God had a definite plan and purpose for his life. Many years later the apostle Paul wrote, "All things work together for good to them that love God." In these words he is expressing the truth which dominated Joseph's life. In our world today, greatness is often measured by the place of prominence which a man has acquired and by the social level which he occupies. Yet greatness in any field is a relative concept. The desire to excel is normal, but there is often a discrepancy between true and false greatness, and true and false values. Real greatness is often overlooked but in the case of Joseph it was openly honored.

In the Book of Genesis as we have studied man's relationship to God, and God's dealings with men, a true idea of greatness is brought to our minds. God looks into the hearts of men. He is not impressed by outward greatness. When He sees faith and love and trust in a man's heart, He counts this for righteousness. In the case of Abraham, the Bible gives no description of his physical stature. We find no words that would indicate that he was more intelligent or more astute than other men of his day. The one outstanding thing which the Scriptures reveal about Abraham is his faith. "Abraham believed God and this was counted to him for righteousness." Abraham "looked for a city whose builder and maker is God." He was called the "friend of

God" who sought to please God in all he did. We are reminded of the words of our Lord, "I do always the things that please my Father."

In the great crises of his life Jacob turned to God. His life was not as exemplary as that of Joseph, but his trust in God was rewarded, and he was blessed by Him. Jacob dealt with Esau for his birthright. He did connive with his mother to deceive his blind father for the blessing which he wanted to have. When Jacob fled from his brother Esau, God appeared to him in the vision of the ladder which stood upon the earth and reached into heaven, with angels ascending and descending upon it. Here again God promised to Jacob His blessing. We may not approve of Jacob, but God, who looks into the heart of man, saw something in this man which merited His blessing. During his lost years of servitude under Laban, who changed his wages countless times, God was with Jacob and blessed him with cattle and sheep and camels in great numbers. His greatest sorrow came when he was told that Joseph, Rachel's son, was dead. His greatest joy came when he found that Joseph his beloved son was alive. We can readily appreciate his joy when he was given this wonderful message from the son whom he had thought to be dead and for whom he had mourned so many years.

> Haste ye, and go up to my father, and say unto him, Thus saith thy son Joseph, God hath made me lord of all Egypt: come down unto me, tarry not: And thou shalt dwell in the land of Goshen, and thou shalt be near unto me, thou, and thy children, and thy children's children, and thy flocks, and thy herds, and all that thou hast (Gen. 45:9-10).

When it was told to Pharaoh that Joseph's brothers had come, he and his servants were delighted at the news. Pharaoh urged Joseph to send for his father and all his household and offered them the best the land had to offer. Pharaoh himself sought to meet the Hebrew patriarch. "And Jacob blessed Pharaoh." It is not hard to picture the oriental monarch in his royal robes and in his magnificent surroundings, nor to feel the quiet dignity of Jacob, a man of wealth and renown in his own land, raising his hand in blessing upon Pharaoh. In the Book of Hebrews it is written, "Without all contradiction the less is blest of the better." This places Jacob on a higher plane than Pharaoh. We might ask, "How can this possibly be true?" Let us not forget that Jacob who had "prevailed" when he clung to the angel of the Lord for blessing had been so profoundly blessed that his name was changed to Israel. The record is that he "walked with God" so he was at all times in the presence of the Creator and the Sovereign of heaven and earth.

Chapter Twenty-four

THE FAITH OF THE PATRIARCHS

(Genesis 46-50)

> And it came to pass after these things, that one told
> Joseph, Behold, thy father is sick (Gen. 48:1).

Immediately Joseph called to him his two sons, Ephraim
and Manasseh, and hastened with them to his father's bedside. When they entered Jacob's room he revived and sat
up in bed. He reviewed before Joseph and his sons the
wonderful way in which almighty God had appeared to him
in the land of Canaan. He told them of the way he had been
blessed. Now that he was dying he wanted to pronounce
God's blessing on Joseph and his sons. He motioned the
two boys to come near to his bed and then he kissed and
embraced them. "And Israel said unto Joseph, I had not
thought to see thy face: and, lo, God hath shewed me also
thy seed" (48:11). What a great blessing to have spent the
last seventeen years of his life near Joseph, to see him in a
place of such great prominence and to see Ephraim and
Manasseh grow up into young manhood!

> And he blessed Joseph, and said, God, before whom my
> fathers Abraham and Isaac did walk, the God which fed
> me all my life long unto this day, the Angel which re-
> deemed me from all evil, bless the lads; and let my name
> be named on them, and the name of my fathers Abraham
> and Isaac; and let them grow into a multitude in the
> midst of the earth (48:15-16).

As Jacob laid his hands in blessing on the heads of
Joseph's sons, Joseph noticed that his father's right hand

rested on the head of Ephraim his younger son, so he held up his father's right hand to place it on Manasseh's head, and said, "Not so, my father, for this is the firstborn." But his father said, "I know it, my son . . . but truly his younger brother shall be greater than he." And Israel said unto Joseph, "Behold, I die: but God shall be with you, and bring you again unto the land of your fathers."

After this all the sons of Jacob came to the bedside of their dying father, and he had a special word for each one of them, from Reuben his oldest to Benjamin his youngest. The tribes of Israel are not identical with the sons of Jacob: there is no mention of a tribe of Joseph, but Ephraim and Manasseh are included in the twelve tribes. This would have made thirteen but the tribe of Levi did not receive an inheritance in the Promised Land, because the men of this tribe were chosen and ordained by God to serve as priests and levites and porters and singers in the tabernacle. They were given cities to dwell in and received the tithes which the children of Israel brought to the Lord, and so this tribe was not included among the tribes who received the land of Canaan as their inheritance.

> And when Jacob had made an end of commanding his sons, he gathered up his feet into the bed, and yielded up the ghost, and was gathered unto his people (49:33).

After many days of mourning, Joseph and his brothers and the whole household of Israel set out for Canaan to bury the body of Jacob their father. They were accompanied by "all the servants of Pharaoh, the elders of his house, and all the elders of the land of Egypt. . . . And there went up with him both chariots and horsemen: and it was a very great company. . . . And his sons did unto him according as he commanded them: for his sons carried him into the land of Canaan." They buried his body in the cave in which Abraham and Sarah and Isaac and Rebekah were buried. The deep regard in which Jacob was held by his sons and their families was a bond of loyalty and love which united the family in their faith in God. This is an example of how the life of faith of a godly man carries over to his children and grandchildren. No child develops into a believer because of the faith of his father, but a child who has the example of a believing parent before him will be more responsive to the call of God. Whenever the Word of God is implanted in the heart, it will produce blessing.

The Bible tells of both blessing and cursing. What does this really mean? This can be understood if we look at a garden. When we plant beans in our garden and we harvest more beans, we could say that we have been blessed. When weeds come up and produce more weeds, we would say that we have been cursed. In this way the increase of beans can be likened to blessing, and the increase of weeds can be likened to cursing. Sowing the Word of God in the heart of a child will always produce blessing, but the Word will not increase automatically. It must be sown and cultivated and nurtured. It is true that so very much depends upon the way in which a child is brought up. His training will be a vital factor when he responds to accept the Gospel and thereby be blessed, or to reject it and be under condemnation. If I am going to harvest beans, I will need to plant them. If we want our children to grow up as believers, we will need to plant the Gospel. What is true in the physical is also true in the spiritual.

Bringing an infant to the Lord in baptism, and promising to bring it up in the nurture and the admonition of the Lord is vital. It is important that parents supply all the physical needs of their children, as well as to train them in proper ethics and morals and conduct. How much more important that these children be trained in spiritual things! The Scriptures make it clear that parents are responsible for the spiritual welfare of their children, even though parents cannot coerce them to believe in God. Parents who read the Bible and pray in the presence of their children, and take them to Sunday school, give their children much more than worldly riches. Genesis presents the record of the blessing which God gave to Abraham and Isaac and Jacob. That this blessing was given individually is true, yet Isaac and Jacob had the deep abiding faith in God which had been so evident in the lives of their respective fathers.

Faith in God was the greatest heritage Jacob left to his sons. Many may find it hard to accept that the truths of the Bible are eternal, and "forever settled in the heavens." But the lessons to be learned in the Book of Genesis that speak of God's dealings with men are as valid today as they were hundreds and thousands of years ago. The faith of Abraham, the wisdom of Isaac, and the persistence of Jacob in seeking God's blessing are a never failing source of spiritual enrichment to all who read this book.

The life and career of Joseph have often been spoken of as typical of Christ, foreshadowing the revelation that was to come. As Isaac was the son of promise, so Joseph was an answer to years of prayer. We read that God remembered Rachel and hearkened to her prayer and granted her and Jacob a son. Joseph was greatly beloved of his father. When Jesus of Nazareth was baptized in the river Jordan, a voice from heaven said, "This is my beloved Son in whom I am well pleased." Joseph was obedient and reliable and trustworthy. He pleased his father in all that he did. Jesus of Nazareth could say, "I do all things to please my Father." Joseph was hated and envied by his brothers. We read that our Lord Jesus Christ came unto His own, and His own received Him not. Joseph's brothers had it in mind to kill him. The Pharisees went about seeking how they might destroy our Lord. Joseph was sold by his brothers as a slave for twenty pieces of silver. Jesus of Nazareth was sold by one of his own disciples for thirty pieces of silver. One of the peculiar sorrows of Jesus of Nazareth was that a man who had been in His company for so long betrayed Him. Joseph was faithful as a servant and yet he was falsely accused. Our Lord was brought into the court of the High Priest and convicted on false evidence. Joseph was put into prison and was released and given a place of power and honor. Jesus our Lord was buried in the grave and raised from the dead into victory and glory and triumph. How wonderful to find that the life of one of the patriarchs of the Old Testament foreshadowed the pattern of the earthly life of our Lord! Even as Joseph delivered his whole family from famine and brought them into a place of plenty, so

Christ delivers all who believe in Him from eternal death. All who will believe and receive this truth may enter into the glories of heaven. What a wealth of information and instruction there is for us in the Book of Genesis! Reading and studying this book enables a person to comprehend more fully the New Testament Scripture.